FAMOUS
FASHION
DESIGNERS

MARC JACOBS

FAMOUS FASHION DESIGNERS

COCO CHANEL

MARC JACOBS

CALVIN KLEIN

RALPH LAUREN

STELLA McCARTNEY

ISAAC MIZRAHI

VALENTINO

VERSACE

FAMOUS
FASHION
DESIGNERS

MARC JACOBS

Mary Boone

CHELSEA HOUSE
An Infobase Learning Company

MARC JACOBS

Copyright © 2011 by Infobase Learning

Chelsea House
An imprint of Infobase Learning
132 West 31st Street
New York NY 10001

Library of Congress Cataloging-in-Publication Data

Boone, Mary.
　Marc Jacobs / by Mary Boone.
　　p. cm. — (Famous fashion designers)
　Includes bibliographical references and index.
　ISBN 978-1-60413-981-5 (hardcover)
　1. Jacobs, Marc, 1963-—Juvenile literature. 2. Fashion designers—United States—
Biography—Juvenile literature. I. Jacobs, Marc, 1963- II. Title.
　TT505.J32B66 2011
　746.9'2092—dc22
　　　　　　　　　　　　　　　　2010036188

Chelsea House books are available at special discounts when purchased in bulk quantities for businesses, associations, institutions, or sales promotions. Please call our Special Sales Department in New York at (212) 967-8800 or (800) 322-8755.

You can find Chelsea House on the World Wide Web at
http://www.chelseahouse.com

Text design by Lina Farinella
Composition by EJB Publishing Services
Cover design by Alicia Post
Cover printed by Bang Printing, Brainerd, Minn.
Book printed and bound by Bang Printing, Brainerd, Minn.
Date printed: March 2011
Printed in the United States of America

10 9 8 7 6 5 4 3 2 1

Contents

1

Perfect
Beginnings

Marc Jacobs got his first tattoo in 2006. In the years since then, he's amassed an expansive collection of body art that includes SpongeBob SquarePants, the M&M's mascot, stars, a couch, nuzzling pups, a *Simpsons* cartoon version of himself, and more than two dozen other designs.

Of all this ink, one of the most notable images is scrawled across his right wrist: the word *Perfect*. "I put it there to remind me, for when I'm looking at myself and wishing that I could be strong in this way or better at that thing, and I can just say, 'No, I'm exactly how I need to be,' So, perfect," he told the *New Yorker* in 2009.

Jacobs, now one of the world's most prominent fashion designers and eminent rule-breakers, has not always been so confident and self-assured. Born April 9, 1963, his Manhattan childhood was punctuated with sadness and instability. Jacobs's father, a talent agent, died when he was seven. His mother, whom Jacobs calls "a mess," remarried three times and moved the family from New Jersey to Long Island to the Bronx. She checked herself in and out of hospitals. Finally, when he was a teenager, Jacobs decided he'd had enough.

He moved in with his paternal grandmother on New York's Upper West Side. His grandmother traveled extensively and loved the finer things in life. She enjoyed spending time with her grandson and even taught him to knit. "I always say I lived my life with my grandmother," he told the *New York Times Magazine* in 2005. "She was emotionally stable and she was very encouraging to me."

When Jacobs's grandmother died in 1987, he cut ties to the rest of his family. "Living with my grandmother, I just kind of grew up feeling like I'm not going to be obliged to spend Thanksgiving with a bunch of people I didn't like—or who didn't like me," he told the *New Yorker* in 2008. "I shouldn't do anything or shouldn't feel anything. I either do feel or I don't feel. I'm not going to 'should' feel."

Jacobs is more matter-of-fact than melancholy when he talks about his less-than-traditional childhood. "I look at the positive side of all the negative things that happened to me," he told *Out* magazine in 2007. "That again, is a choice of perspective. I've only learned in the past decade how important that sense of perspective can be. My sister and brother and I all grew up under the same circumstances, and I don't think it strengthened them in the way it strengthened me, but then, others would look at my strengths as weaknesses."

Jacobs's interest in fashion goes back to his early childhood. "I used to go to sleep-away camp, and they'd provide a list of things that you had to bring, and I always wanted to be a bit more creative than the list allowed," he said in *The Teen Vogue Handbook* in 2009. "Like, if they required chinos, I wanted to hand-paint them. Even then, I thought of clothes as a way to express oneself, as a kind of theatre."

Making Halloween costumes was a treat for the budding designer. What could be better than using a needle and thread to bring fantasy to life? He used scissors and beads and paints to give old fashions new looks. Not having a lot of money to spend on fabrics or supplies never stopped him. In fact, it probably forced him to become more resourceful. "I'd go to a uniform store and buy an air-conditioner-repairman jumpsuit and then customize it," he said in *The Teen Vogue Handbook*. "I'd buy carpenter's pants and overdye them or a sweatshirt and cut off the sleeves. That way I could achieve the look I wanted."

Jacobs attended the High School of Art and Design in New York City and got an after-school job as a stock boy at the influential New York boutique Charivari. Even when he was promoted to folding shirts and sweaters, the work wasn't glamorous. But it was important. He learned fabrics, he learned what looks good on certain body types, and he began to make connections with industry insiders. It was at Charivari that he met designer Perry Ellis, who Jacobs says encouraged him to attend Parsons the New School for Design and then mentored him while he was a student.

When Jacobs was 15, his uncle, the president of the William Morris Agency, arranged for him to work in the talent agency's mail room. His was a childhood without restrictions, so he took advantage of talent agents' offers to get him on guest lists at music shows. "I met an agent who was covering music there and he would get me on guest lists even though I was too young," Jacobs told *Rolling Stone* in 2008. "I would get turned on by a band's look first and, once I did, I found I actually liked the music."

It was not uncommon for a teenage Jacobs to go to clubs like Hurrah or Studio 54 all night long, sometimes bringing his backpack so he could go straight to class the next morning. That early exposure to cutting-edge music had a lasting influence. Jacobs's fashion shows often include rock concert–inspired production elements, and his advertising campaigns have featured musicians, including White Stripes drummer Meg White and English singer/songwriter M.I.A.

 Even at a young age, Marc Jacobs's talent for fashion and art were obvious. Perry Ellis, a famous designer in the 1980s, encouraged Jacobs to enroll at Parsons the New School for Design.

Being an underage devotee of nightclubs also played a role in Jacobs's accelerated route toward maturity; as a teen, he began taking drugs and drinking heavily. He also had an awakening about his sexuality at a fairly young age. He was at an overnight summer camp when he realized he wasn't like the other kids. He didn't want to play football, drive fast cars, or sneak into the girls' cabins; instead, he preferred arts and crafts time and developed a crush on his counselor. "I was always teased by other kids for being gay before I'd ever had any kind of sexual contact with another man, and I was always afraid of what it meant (to be gay), but I was also very excited by it," he told *Out* magazine in 2005.

DESIGNS ON DESIGN

Post high school, Jacobs followed Ellis's advice and attended Parsons. While there, he designed his first collection of hand-knit sweaters commissioned and sold by Barbara Weiser under the label Marc Jacobs for Marc and Barbara. The sweaters were sold at the Weiser family's Charivari stores.

Jacobs designed and hand knit three similarly oversized, very heavy sweaters as the centerpiece of his senior-year fashion show at Parsons. In the spring of 1984, Jacobs showed his senior collection and was ultimately honored with the fashion school's highest awards: the Perry Ellis Gold Thimble, the Chester Weinberg Gold Thimble, and Design Student of the Year.

Having seen Jacobs's sweaters at Charivari, *New York Times* photographer Bill Cunningham featured them in his Sunday "On the Street" column. Suddenly, people were talking about this hip, young designer with the uncanny ability to combine elegance and comfort.

Bang! Jacobs's career was taking off in a big way.

CATCHING THE RIGHT PERSON'S EYE

Perhaps even more notable is the fact that Jacobs met businessperson Robert Duffy at his senior fashion show. "He was working for

Getting Schooled

Marc Jacobs studied his craft at Parsons the New School for Design in New York City. Founded in 1896, Parsons has been churning out outstanding artists, designers, and business leaders for more than a century.

Parsons' School of Fashion is among the world's most renowned design programs. Fashion-related courses are taught at the David M. Schwartz Fashion Education Center, in the heart of the city's Garment District, an area of Seventh Avenue where many of the nation's most prominent designers have their showrooms and studios.

Parsons students take classes related to fashion drawing, machine knitting, themes in fashion history, production, sustainability, and distribution. Students devote most of their senior year to a thesis project. Students develop three collection concepts, one of which is selected for completion and presented to a jury of industry professionals. In conjunction with the thesis project, students develop a portfolio and participate in several high-level competitions. Collections are photographed and presented in the school's online Look Book.

In the spring of 2010, Parsons administrators announced the establishment of two new fashion graduate programs: a studio-based master of fine arts degree in fashion design and society, initiated through the support of designer and alumna Donna Karan, and a master's degree in fashion studies.

Beyond Jacobs and Karan, Parsons has played a key role in launching the careers of many top American designers past and present, including Claire McCardell, Adrian, Norman Norell, Tom Ford, and Narciso Rodriguez.

Behnaz Sarafpour, Doo Ri, Vena Cava, Ohne Titel, and Proenza Schouler designers Lazaro Hernandez and Jack McCollough—who met at Parsons—are among a new generation of global designers who have studied at Parsons.

Support from people like Robert Duffy and Anna Wintour (*above*) helped Jacobs acquire the financial backing and the publicity needed to maintain a successful fashion business. With their help, Jacobs rocketed to the top of the fashion industry.

a Seventh Avenue company that wanted to start a 'contemporary' line of clothing," Jacobs told *Index* magazine in 2001. "Robert convinced them to hire me right out of school." Theirs is a partnership that continues to this day.

Sharing the belief that no one was making high fashion for young, cool people, Jacobs and Duffy combined forces to form Jacobs Duffy Designs. They set up a small studio in the Garment District; Jacobs consulted for other brands, including Iceberg and Kashiyama, to earn extra cash.

Almost from the start, Jacobs's panache and creativity caught the attention of those in the fashion industry. He had a knack for making expensive clothes look casual, which at the time was a brand-new concept. Jacobs and Duffy's fledging design business was surviving thanks to the support of some very key people. Longtime *Vogue* magazine editor Anna Wintour, for example, lauded Jacobs's designs. Buyers at upscale department stores such as Bergdorf Goodman and Bloomingdale's placed big orders. And supermodels Naomi Campbell, Linda Evangelista, and Christy Turlington volunteered to model in his runway shows—for free.

While most young designers struggle for years as pattern makers or sketching assistants yearning for recognition, Marc Jacobs was very quickly becoming an industry darling. Still, in spite of the incredible celebrity support and praise from critics, Jacobs Duffy Designs spent those first few years teetering between success and failure. Finances were tight, deadlines were missed, and the company was plagued by both theft and fire.

Through it all, Jacobs and Duffy never gave up. "There has never been one moment when I thought we would fail," said Duffy in a 2005 *New York Times Magazine* interview about the team's success.

Tragedy at another design house—Perry Ellis International—turned to eventual triumph for Jacobs. Ellis was at the peak of his career when he died in 1986 at age 46. Though no one

After the death of designer Perry Ellis (*above*, with actress Mariel Hemingway), many worried that his company would fail without his leadership. Jacobs and Duffy were brought on board to help the business regain its foothold in the industry.

would confirm that his death was related to AIDS, some newspaper reports suggested Ellis was a victim of the disease. At the time, there were fears—fueled primarily by misunderstanding

---

ELEMENTS OF STYLE

It's not about fashion, it's about style.

> —*Marc Jacobs at the close of his New York Winter Runway Show, 2010*

What's comfortable to me is familiarity. Comfort has nothing to do with the size of the garment. I do find something quite comfortable and charming in a too-narrow shoulder, a sleeve that's too short or too long, a pant that's too high or too low, hems that are trod on.

> —*Marc Jacobs in* New York *magazine, 2005*

---

and misinformation—that AIDS could be contracted by casual contact. The *Daily News Record*, a well-known menswear publication, reported that rumors of Ellis's AIDS diagnosis had hurt sales because some consumers were afraid they might contract the disease by simply touching a Perry Ellis dress or wearing a Perry Ellis blouse.

At the time of Ellis's death, the company was generating $750 million a year in sales. Clearly, the challenge was to keep Perry Ellis International afloat without the guidance of its namesake designer. Two longtime Ellis assistants were promoted and took over design responsibilities for the company's menswear and women's wear lines. It wasn't long, though, before sales began to falter, and the decision was made to bring in outside talent.

In 1988, Perry Ellis design house hired Roger Forsythe to oversee its menswear division. The company also took a chance on a couple of newcomers; Jacobs and Duffy joined Perry Ellis as vice president of women's design and president, respectively. Sure, Jacobs would be designing under another name, but Jacobs and Duffy finally had the financing and infrastructure they'd longed for. Everything was finally going to be perfect. Or not.

2

From Ellis
to Vuitton

Landing at Perry Ellis was the fulfillment of a dream for business partners Marc Jacobs and Robert Duffy. Finally, they had the financial backing and infrastructure they'd longed for—even if it meant designing under another name. Of course, the new job also brought with it an enormous amount of pressure, which Jacobs dealt with by drinking and using drugs. He worried about failing, but he designed without fear. His collections drew inspiration from the past and were updated with irony and intelligence.

"I was told my first collection wasn't Perry Ellis enough," Jacobs told *Interview* magazine in 2008. "The second was too lady-ish. So, what I learned was that the work that I was proudest of was when I stopped listening to everybody and just responded to what was in my heart." At the time, grunge music was in his heart. And it inspired a 1992 collection that people still talk about all these years later.

Jacobs was fascinated by bands such as Nirvana, Alice in Chains, Pearl Jam, and Soundgarden. The bands, many based out of the Seattle, Washington, area, produced a type of music called grunge, known for its heavy guitar sounds and straightforward, high-energy performances. Lyrics typically addressed social issues such as apathy, confinement, and a desire for freedom. Grunge bands often rejected the high-tech, overly produced sound of other genres. Shows didn't include a lot of the light shows and smoke effects other rock concerts of the era included. Musicians looked more like blue-collar workers than superstars, often wearing dirty, ripped jeans, flannel shirts, and uncombed hair. It was a type of music that fused elements of several genres but defied definition, and that's why Jacobs liked it.

"I thought this music was just so incredible because it reminded me of when I was younger and punk rock was really, again, something none of us had ever heard before, it just was a new thing," Jacobs told broadcaster Charlie Rose in 1998. "The sound coming out of Seattle—grunge—had that same sort of shock."

Grunge music and clothing inspired Jacobs's 1992 collection. Proportions were awkward; skirts and tops were too long or too short, shrunken or oversized. Patterns and fabrics clashed. The unexpected combinations excited some viewers but shocked others. Thermal underwear was reimagined in cashmere. Pretty floral dresses were paired with clunky combat boots and cro-cheted skullcaps. Birkenstock sandals were made in satin and Chuck Taylor sneakers in silk. Flowing button-up skirts were left unbuttoned to reveal hot pants, and $300 silk shirts were printed to look like flannel.

"I wanted to create a collection that basically was visual noise," Jacobs said of the collection on PBS's *The Charlie Rose Show*. "So we clashed patterns and stripes and colors and textures and we layered it. Girls were wearing 10 layers of clothes, of course they were all very fine; it was silk chiffons over laces over whatever, so it was a very deluxe version of this grunge attitude. But, again, I didn't originally start out to do grunge, I just wanted to create some kind of visual noise by clashing patterns."

Critics mostly applauded the disheveled looks and cheered Jacobs for forcing women to rethink fashion. Perry Ellis executives did not share the critics' enthusiasm and weren't convinced women would spend a lot of money for designer clothes that looked like they came from a secondhand store. They fired Jacobs and Duffy shortly after the release of the collection.

The Other Half of the Jacobs-Duffy Partnership

When Robert Duffy married Paraguay native Alex Cespedes in April 2010, Marc Jacobs served as the best man. That's the way Duffy and Jacobs's relationship has worked for more than a quarter of a century. They're business partners and more; they've seen each other through hirings and firings, good times and bad. The powerful pair are owners, along with LVMH Moët Hennessy-Louis Vuitton S.A., of the Marc Jacobs label, and they are directors at Louis Vuitton, where Jacobs designs the clothes, shoes, and bags.

"Marc Jacobs is not Marc Jacobs," Jacobs told *Fortune* magazine in 2007. "Marc Jacobs is Marc Jacobs and Robert Duffy or Robert Duffy and Marc Jacobs, whichever way you want to put it."

Duffy grew up the son of a steel industry executive in a small town in western Pennsylvania. He moved to New York City after high school and became the first man to work the sales floor at the high-end store Bergdorf Goodman, where he learned that he excelled at selling things. He was a 30-year-old sales manager for Seventh Avenue manufacturer Reuben Thomas when he saw Jacobs's senior show at

Down but not out, the fashion duo took their severance pay from Perry Ellis and rented a store on New York's Mercer Street. They set up a tiny studio with a pattern maker and two seamsters. Money was tight, but they were able to produce small shows. "So many wonderful people in the fashion industry were there to support us—that was a great help for me," Jacobs told *Women's Wear Daily* in 2010. "[Italian designers] Gianni Versace and Donatella Versace came to our first show."

Individually, Jacobs and Duffy were approached with job offers, but they turned them down, one after another. At different times, they both considered giving up, but Duffy says he never forgot the

Parsons School of Design. The two got funding from Reuben Thomas in 1984 (a year Duffy has tattooed on his hand), and they've been winding their way—together—through the fashion world ever since.

Gail Zauder, managing partner of the specialty investment bank Elixir Advisors, which has brokered major deals with some of the world's most recognizable fashion houses, says Jacobs is a "phenomenon" but notes it is not his talent alone that separates him from his competitors. "He just had a guy that knew how to commercialize his business better, and that guy is Robert Duffy," she told *Fortune* in 2007.

While Jacobs's focus clearly is on design, Duffy's is on the duo's stores. He is concerned with sales figures, customer demographics, location, and display, and he has been known to spend hours in their stores obsessing over details such as folding and stocking merchandise. The success of their partnership, says Jacobs, is based on mutual respect and admiration. "Robert appreciates what I do," he told *Out* magazine in 2005. "He doesn't try to change it."

Duffy—more than any blood relative—has become Jacobs's family. "We were in business a long time before LVMH," Duffy told the *New York Times* in 2006. "When young designers ask me, I say we were extremely lucky that we had each other. We have unconditional love and trust for each other. We started on a handshake. We are always there to protect each other. And Marc knows he will always get the truth from me."

advice he received from Gianni Versace. "He said to me, 'Whatever you do, do not split up,'" Duffy told *Out* magazine in 2005. "You cannot go through this industry alone and survive."

ENTERING THE WORLD OF LOUIS VUITTON

The two continued to believe in Jacobs's designs. Then, in 1996, the duo got a call from French businessperson Bernard Arnault, the founder, chair, and chief executive officer of Moët Hennessy-Louis Vuitton (LVMH), a group of more than 50 luxury brands. Arnault had been busy matching trendsetting designers, including Alexander McQueen, John Galliano, and Narciso Rodriguez, with traditional French design houses such as Givenchy, Christian Dior, and Loewe. Now, he wanted to meet Jacobs and Duffy and see their clothes; he wanted to talk to them about the top jobs at Dior or Givenchy.

Initially, Duffy didn't want to get Jacobs's hopes up, so he waited a while even to tell him about the call. And, as Duffy told *New York* magazine in 2005, "We didn't want to have to follow another designer; we'd done that at Perry Ellis." Soon, though, the two were flown to Paris to meet with Arnault. During that meeting, Duffy suggested he and Jacobs might be a good fit for Louis Vuitton, a company famous for its handbags and trunks but which had no ready-to-wear line.

Arnault, Duffy, and Jacobs talked about the possibilities for nearly a year and a half. Initially, Arnault didn't want to hire Duffy as part of the deal. Then, Jacobs and Duffy insisted that if they were to head up Louis Vuitton, they should also get financing for Jacobs's own line. At first, Arnault balked at the idea, but he later agreed to invest just enough in the Marc Jacobs label so they could open their Mercer Street store and produce clothes for a few runway shows. Finally, in 1997, negotiations were complete, and Jacobs and Duffy signed on with LVMH's Louis Vuitton.

The relationship has not always been easy. There were ongoing power struggles and countless disagreements over finances and staffing. The pressure to succeed was overwhelming, and it kicked Jacobs's dependency on drugs and alcohol into high gear.

Executives at Perry Ellis were unhappy with Jacobs's new look for the company and fired him and Duffy. The two found another, more creative partnership with Louis Vuitton. *Above,* Jacobs greets the audience after his fall/winter 1998 Louis Vuitton show.

"This Vuitton thing was scary," Jacobs said in 2008 during a speech at Central Saint Martins, one of the United Kingdom's most prestigious fashion schools. "Suddenly you're on the Paris stage with this huge name. I felt so paralyzed by it. That first collection was a no-win situation. I thought, if I give them what they expect, they'll be disappointed because they want to be surprised. If I give them a surprise, they'll be disappointed it wasn't what they were expecting."

Once he finally settled in and gained a little confidence, Jacobs set out to reinvent Louis Vuitton's image with fashionable ready-to-wear and accessories collections. Some of his earliest successes came about by introducing seasonal collaborations that updated the company's traditional beige-on-brown *LV* design logo. The logo was such an important part of Vuitton's image and reputation that he knew he couldn't get rid of it or even alter it drastically, so he started to think about new ways to showcase the famous letters.

Jacobs was visiting the home of actress, singer, and songwriter Charlotte Gainsbourg in Paris when inspiration struck. "She had, by the side of her bed, a Louis Vuitton trunk that had been painted black by her father, and the monogram was sort of peeking through," he told *Harper's Bazaar* in 2008. Moved by that image, and the work of French artist Marcel Duchamp, who famously drew a funny little beard and mustache on Leonardo da Vinci's *Mona Lisa*, Jacobs began to think about ways in which he could add life to the traditional *LV*.

"It's about taking something that's very iconic and revered and defacing it and creating something new, somewhat rebellious, and kind of punk," he told *Harper's Bazaar*, noting it took a while to convince Vuitton executives that marring the popular bags was a good idea.

In 2001, Jacobs teamed up with artist/fashion designer Stephen Sprouse to release Vuitton's classic monogram bag scrawled with Sprouse's graffiti. Initially, Vuitton management thought the bags, known as Speedy Graffiti, might be used only on the runway or in advertisements, but consumer demand was overwhelming. Waiting lists to buy the bags were created, and thousands of the bags were produced.

Hoping to reinvigorate the Louis Vuitton brand, Jacobs collaborated with several designers to create a line of "LV" bags that combined the classic logo with a modern, edgier look.

This updated Vuitton bag appealed to new customers and generated more than $300 million in sales during its debut year. It also signaled the beginning of partnerships with the likes of Japanese pop artist Takashi Murakami and American painter and photographer Richard Prince, each triumphantly adding flair to a once-staid bag. Murakami brought the *LV* monogram to life in 33 clashing colors against a black or white background; his later designs incorporated cartoonish pink cherry blossoms. Prince created splashy, colorful bags, some of which included the silk-screened *LV* logo on canvas along with jokes inspired by old Vaudeville acts; on others, Prince created cartoons that were hand embroidered on boldly colored bags. The collaborations have been so successful that the greatest challenge has been combatting the regularity with which fake Louis Vuitton bags are produced and sold online and on street corners around the world.

Jacobs and his team have spent more than a decade building the hipness quotient of Louis Vuitton bags and clothes, during which time the company's fashion business has quadrupled. While styles change from season to season, the brand always has a luxurious feel, often built on expert tailoring, fine fabrics, and lots of embellishment. The lasting success of the collection gives Jacobs peace of mind. That he has been able to serve as Louis Vuitton's creative director at the same time he was building Marc Jacobs into a fashion empire has earned him the respect of both colleagues

ELEMENTS OF STYLE

I often feel uncomfortable. I have this feeling like this is only going to be good as long as it's good. Am I always full of ideas? No. Those things don't happen every six months. It's not even like, You have to change the shape of handbags and the luxury market. It's like, This has to change the shape of history. And I don't know how to calculate that. I really don't.

—*Marc Jacobs in* New York *magazine, 2005*

My approach to art is exactly the same as my approach to fashion: straightforward and anti-intellectual.

—*Marc Jacobs in* Harper's Bazaar, *2009*

Designers are always saying they're going to do a collection for women, but then every girl on the runway (catwalk) is under twenty. I wanted a variety of ages and sizes. We set out to cast gorgeous women, women who feel happy to put their make-up on, get dressed up and get all their accessories. It's a bit old-fashioned, I know, but I think it's nice for a change.

—*Marc Jacobs about his Winter 2010–2011 Louis Vuitton show in London's* Telegraph, *2010*

and critics. He is quick to point out the accomplishment is not his alone, crediting his teams of designers, pattern cutters, seamsters, stylists, assistants, public relations people, and others. Many individuals have input and work on every single design. Team members bounce ideas off each other and sift through the chaff to ensure only the best concepts are put into production.

Is he the final filter?

"In a certain way, I am," he told the *Independent* in 2008. "But the customer is the final, final filter. What survives the whole process is what people wear. I'm not interested in making clothes that end up in some dusty museum. I'm interested in clothes people want, covet, desire, wear, use, love, tear, soil. . . . Clothes mean nothing until someone lives in them."

3

Sizzling, Fizzling, Sizzling Again

It seems Marc Jacobs has the golden touch. Everything he designs, from clothes and handbags to shoes and belts, quickly becomes *the* item everyone must have.

In 1987, Jacobs became the youngest designer ever to be awarded the fashion industry's highest honor, the Council of Fashion Designers of America (CFDA) Perry Ellis Award for New Fashion Talent. In the years since, he's won three CFDA tributes for Womenswear Designer of the Year, three Accessory Designer of the Year awards, one award for Menswear Designer of the Year, and an International Award for his work for Louis Vuitton. Whether it's well-tailored striped pantsuits, double-breasted satin coats, or extravagant ball gowns in floral-print taffetas, Jacobs is hot, hot, hot.

Except when he's not.

Jacobs has experienced tremendous success and happiness in both his professional and personal lives. He's also experienced his share of shortcomings. Professionally, Jacobs found himself in the spotlight—and, coincidently the recipient of unwanted criticism—the moment he signed on at Perry Ellis in 1988. His Spring 1993 grunge collection fell flat on Seventh Avenue and got him fired from Perry Ellis. The awkward proportions of his Spring 2005 collection polarized the fashion establishment. Critics called it "brilliant" and "exciting"; retailers said the fullness of the skirts and tops made the clothes unappealing to all but the tallest and very thinnest consumers.

His Spring 2010 Marc Jacobs collection won rave reviews from critics. Cathy Horyn of the *New York Times* called it a "free-spirited attack of fashion," while Suzy Menkes, writing for the *International Herald Tribune*, said the show was "exceptional for its imagination, its attention to detail, and its lyrical vision." Reviewing the show for British *Vogue*, Lauren David Peden wrote: "Marc Jacobs is the kind of designer whose talent gives you chills." Still, with all this praise, the collection's wearability came into question. Would what Jacobs was showing on the runways of New York, Paris, and London translate to the streets of middle America? It wasn't the first time critics would question how Jacobs's designs would translate in the real world—and it likely won't be the last.

COPYING NO ONE

Over the years, Jacobs has been criticized for recycling designs— both his own and those belonging to others. He was accused of plagiarism by a man whose father had designed a scarf in the 1950s that was similar to one in Jacobs's Winter 2008 collection. Famed fashion designer Oscar de la Renta has gone so far as to suggest Jacobs is a "copyist."

Jacobs insists he's copying no one but, rather, paying homage to designers and styles he admires. His refined tailoring is a tribute

Although his work in the past has ranged from layered grunge to skintight femininity, Jacobs has an instinct for what works with specific labels. His clothes for Louis Vuitton are much different than the softer, subtler ensembles of his own Marc Jacobs label (*above*).

to Ellis, and his 1985 tight-fitting, sequined minidress recalls Italian designer Elsa Schiaparelli. His affection for the 1960s is evident in the smiley-face sweaters he made as a design student, the billowing balloon sweaters he included in his Fall 1989 collection, and the leather high-waisted skirts he showed as part of his Fall 2009 collection.

Marc Jacobs's designs have celebrated vintage Miami Beach, the comfort and wholesomeness of gingham, the sharp-witted embroidered designs of American interior designer Elsie de Wolfe, the Wild West, and the Academy Awards. His ability to draw on such wide-ranging references caused *New York* magazine to deem him "master of the mash-up."

He has piles of vintage fabrics, album covers from the 1960s, and promotional photos from 30-year-old movies. He scours old issues of *Vogue, Glamour, Elle,* and *Seventeen* magazines, tearing out pages and making notes about anything that might someday be a source of inspiration. "I happen to love referential material, music that refers to something, and anything where the reference is sort of lost and not in your face," Jacobs told the *New York Times* in 2002.

Critic Guy Trebay defended Jacobs's originality in a 2002 *New York Times* column: "Unlike the many brand-name designers who promote the illusion that their output results from a single prodigious creativity, Mr. Jacobs makes no pretense that fashion emerges full blown from the head of one solitary genius."

Tabloid journalists have taken repeated aim at Jacobs, often accusing him of egotism. The spectacle that is his personal life is tracked by a wide audience, some of whom actually care about his work as a designer and others who seem more interested in who he is planning to feature in his next ad campaign or what he wore to the gym.

Speculation about his love life, too, has been the subject of countless newspaper gossip columns. After bouncing from boyfriend to boyfriend for several decades—some of them

considerably younger—Jacobs entered into a long-term relationship with Brazilian advertising executive Lorenzo Martone. Even
media outlets as reputable as the *New York Times* devoted ink to
articles about the couple: Were they married? Did they break up?
Did Martone attend Robert Duffy's wedding with Jacobs? In July
2010, the two put out official word that they were no longer a couple;
the news was picked up by media organizations around the world.

Fashion Week 101

Fashion Week is an industry event—generally about a week long—
during which fashion designers and fashion houses produce runway
shows featuring their latest, greatest collections. Buyers, fashion critics,
and celebrities attend these shows, all looking for the latest trends.

From Cincinnati, Ohio, to Copenhagen, Denmark, Fashion Week
events are held all over the globe. Some Fashion Weeks are very specific. Summer shows in Miami and Rio de Janeiro, for example, are
dedicated to swimwear, while in Portland, Oregon, Fashion Week
showcases eco-friendly designs. Others feature more generalized
shows, with the best of women's, men's, and even children's apparel.
The most prominent Fashion Weeks are held in the fashion capitals of
the world: New York, London, Milan, and Paris.

In the major fashion capitals, Fashion Weeks are held twice each
year. From January to April, designers show off their autumn and winter collections; from September to November, spring and summer collections are showcased. Showing designs so far ahead of the season
allows the press time to preview collections and gives retailers time to
order what they intend to sell.

Fern Mallis, former director of the Council of Fashion Designers of
America, was a major force in getting New York's first Fashion Week
off the ground. Speaking in 2010 to a group at Savannah College of

CELEBRITY STATUS

It is clear Jacobs has achieved a level of celebrity that's unequaled by most of his peers. "There is definitely part of me that just loves the idea that I'm the headline—I do get some weird thrill out of that," he told the *Telegraph* in 2009. "I'm human. I love attention. I like that I get out of that fashion-designer box and become, I don't know, personality box or celebrity box. I love that. It's fun."

Art and Design in Savannah, Georgia, Mallis explained that prior to the creation of New York Fashion Week, designers would host their shows in warehouses and showrooms throughout the city. During one of Michael Kors's shows, the music was so loud that the ceiling started to reverberate and crumble, with chunks of plaster raining down on the models and spectators. "We live for fashion; we don't want to die for it," she told the crowd.

Out of the crumbling plaster disaster evolved the more expansive and more sophisticated event now known as New York Fashion Week. For nearly two decades, New York's Fashion Week designer shows took place in tents in Bryant Park; in the fall of 2010, the shows moved to Lincoln Center. Established fashion houses each produce their own show. Scenes are set with crystal chandeliers or fake brick walls sprayed with graffiti or plain white sets; music further influences the mood. Isaac Mizrahi's 2010 Fall/Winter show, for example, featured leaves hung from the ceiling and even fake snow flurries.

Of course, not every designer gets his or her own show. Some shows feature work by several up-and-coming designers, while other designers host small, off-site shows to coincide with Fashion Week.

In New York alone, more than 250 invitation-only fashion shows attract about 235,000 attendees annually, including buyers for clothing stores, celebrities, reporters, editors, and photographers from more than 35 countries. And, as much as clothing is in the spotlight during Fashion Week, most folks can't help but talk about the celebrities sitting in the front row at each show; Madonna, Lady Gaga, Rihanna, Lindsey Lohan, and the Kardashian sisters are regulars at some of the more prominent shows.

Jacobs began a diffusion line—a moderately priced label that maintains his aesthetic—called Marc by Marc Jacobs (*above*). Designed with mass-market appeal, the clothes are in such demand that there are waiting lists for the boots and handbags.

Of course, the "fun" quotient is minimized when press coverage is negative. The very same reporters who have cheered his designs have also been known to criticize his appearance, his taste in men, and his relapse from sobriety.

Friends say the challenges that have plagued Jacobs have, in some ways, served him well. They argue that he'll hit a low point with his drinking or a relationship and then bounce back, better and stronger than ever before. "It's terrible to say this," artist Elizabeth Peyton told *W* magazine in 2007, "but I think all that pain Marc goes through always brings him so much farther in terms of his ability to create. He's very much like an artist that way. There are all these ideas and influences and conflicts jumbled in his head, and he works through them and arrives at the next place, where you never imagined he'd go."

For many years, Jacobs looked like a complete fashion industry outsider; he was pale and pudgy, had long hair, and always wore thick, nerdy glasses. He smoked constantly, drank soda, and ate fast-food burgers. He was quiet and barely came out on the runway at the end of his shows.

In 2006, he remade himself—almost completely. Daily two-hour workouts have turned his body lean and muscular. He cut sugar, flour, dairy, and caffeine from his diet, opting instead for salads, protein shakes, exercise, and sunshine. He is now tan, with contact lenses and short, purposefully styled hair. He poses for photos—sometimes wearing little more than his underwear—and parades around the runways in a diamond necklace and diamond earrings. Contrary to his devotion to health and wellness, Jacobs admits he still smokes incessantly. It is a total makeover—almost.

The new look and lifestyle have given Jacobs an improved sense of confidence. Feeling good about himself gives him the strength and energy to do more. Jacobs told the *Telegraph* in 2009:

> All of a sudden, before I knew it, I started to say, "Gee, I'm really happy with the work we've been doing." I'm really happy with

the house I live in. I'm really happy with the way I look when I look at myself in the mirror. I spend hours in the bathroom now. I used to spend five minutes! But I like taking a shower. I like shampooing my hair. I like putting on moisturizer. I like wearing jewelry. All of these things I used to think, "That's not for me. I'm on the floor picking up pins or I'm sketching all day. What does it matter what I look like?" And then I discovered—you know what—it does matter. It makes me feel good.

As improved as Jacobs's self-image is, he is the first to admit that doubts linger. He can't seem to shake the notion that failure or collapse is just around the next corner. "I'm as tortured as ever," he told the *Financial Times* in 2010. "I see my shrink once a week,

ELEMENTS OF STYLE

It was never my desire to revolutionize fashion, to make clothes that could be in a museum. I want to create clothes that have a certain style, but I want to see them used. I want to see people enjoy the things I've made.

—*Marc Jacobs in* Teen Vogue Handbook:
An Insider's Guide to Careers in Fashion, *2009*

It's so amazing to me how into fashion the majority of people I come across are. It doesn't really matter what the trend is or what the look is—you've got to have one, so I find it's like a cartoon world out there where everyone's sort of playing dress-up, and that's why I say there are no bad trends. I don't care if you're doing the sleazy suburban look or a nerd look or a jock look. It reminds me of the voguing balls from years ago, where people used to dress to pass as a certain type of person in society. People have always dressed as their idols, but I think we've greater accessibility to how those people look today.

—*Marc Jacobs in* Out *magazine, 2007*

As a longtime fashion powerhouse, the Louis Vuitton brand began developing its signature aesthetic in the time of Napoleon III. Jacobs retains the classic Louis Vuitton look when designing for the label but also updates it by bringing in influences from different eras and sources.

have all the same mood swings, I can sit there the night before a show and think, 'What if they hate it? What if my life is over and I am homeless?' I can catastrophize with the best of them. I have sat over on that couch with (artist) John Currin and he'll say, 'What are you doing?' and I'll say, 'I have no idea,' and then he'll talk about a smile he's repainted 16 times. But I also have a certain amount of self-awareness at this point, and I recognize all those neuroses are just human."

4

Acknowledging Problems, Finding Answers

At an age when his classmates were playing high school sports and sending off college applications, Marc Jacobs was already a nightclub veteran. Over the years, what began as social drinking became hard partying; soon he was drinking and using drugs more days than he wasn't. "It's a cliché, but when I drank I was taller, funnier, smarter, cooler," he told *New York* magazine in 2005.

Over time, Jacobs found it increasingly difficult to function. He forgot things, overslept, and acted irrationally. He was kicked off several airplanes for disruptive behavior, and on more than one occasion, he ended up in a hotel in a vodka-and-cocaine-fueled haze. He was becoming a danger to both himself and others.

There were times he was so hungover that he didn't show up at work for days. When he sobered up and finally made it in to the office, he demanded the staff work through the weekend to make up for lost time—then he wouldn't show up himself, or he'd show up and fall asleep at his desk. "I'd be very drunk in Tokyo with a friend and start a machismo bet over absinthe about who could hold a cigarette to our skin longer," he told *Rolling Stone* in 2008. "Or, when I was taking certain drugs, I would fall asleep holding a cigarette and wake up with burns."

When it looked like Jacobs's drinking might kill both him and his company, his business partner, Robert Duffy, stepped in to save the day. He sweet-talked the staff, buying them gifts and convincing them not to quit, and made excuses to retailers when delivery deadlines were missed. "More than anything, I hurt for him," Duffy told *New York* magazine in 2005. "Marc's my family. I was just becoming overprotective of him."

In 1999, *Vogue* editor Anna Wintour and model Naomi Campbell told Duffy the problem was no longer tolerable; he needed to do something before Jacobs imploded. It took some time, but Duffy and other friends were finally able to persuade Jacobs to get help.

"I didn't want to go to rehab, at first, because I was high out of my mind," Jacobs told *Rolling Stone*. "Naomi, as someone who struggled with her own demons and problems, was able to take me on. I'm sure the root of my problems goes much further back than before I was successful. When I was younger, all the kids I thought were cool smoked cigarettes, my favorite rock stars were heroin addicts and my favorite writers were taking acid. As a kid, what I thought looked cool was very dark and drug oriented."

In rehab, Jacobs first had to admit he had a problem. Then, he met with psychologists, therapists, and other patients to learn how to cope in a manner that wouldn't send him back to drinking or drugs. He was forced to examine his life closely and change habits related to his addictions. It was a difficult process, but he willingly made those lifestyle changes.

The designer sobered up and produced a string of hit collections and achieved even greater fame. Jacobs was back in control

When Jacobs's work began to suffer because of his increased alcohol and drug use, supermodel and friend Naomi Campbell stepped in and persuaded the young designer to seek treatment. *Above,* Jacobs and Campbell attend one of Jacobs's famous Christmas parties.

and taking care of business, but he wasn't taking care of himself. He smoked nonstop, ate junk food, and developed ulcerative colitis, a bowel disease that caused painful cramps and often left him unable to get out of bed. The colitis was cause for special concern because his father had died of complications related to the same disease. Jacobs coped with the pain the best he could, but there were days it was simply debilitating. He was so uncomfortable that he missed work and personal engagements.

Initially, he tried to cure the ailment with medicine, but the side effects were almost as bad as the disease itself. Finally, he decided to take charge of his health and sought the advice of a nutritionist, who prescribed exercise, naps, a daily dose of sunshine, and a diet with no sugar, dairy, caffeine, or flour.

"Instead of Wendy's five times a day at weird hours and Coca-Cola after Coca-Cola, now I'm drinking six bottles of water, green vegetable juice, and wheat-grass shots with ginger," he told *Rolling Stone*. His diet improved, and he adapted a fitness regimen that quickly became legend throughout the fashion industry; with much work and dedication, he went from fat to fit. It was impossible not to notice Jacobs's physical transformation, and he reveled in showing off his new body. He tanned and wore expensive jewelry for the first time in his life.

But around November 2005, the designer started drinking again. First, it was a couple of drinks while on a business trip to Russia; then, he got drunk while working in Hong Kong. "Well, I wasn't drinking or drugging daily or anything like that," he told *Out* magazine in 2007. "When I first went into rehab in 2000, I really had a horrible problem. I was a daily drug user and abusing alcohol and I went (to rehab) against my will."

Still, Jacobs and his crew were wise enough to know that even periodic drinking is a problem for an addict. "As anyone who has a problem with drinking and drugging knows, it's a steady progression," he told *Out* in 2007. "It's like someone who goes off their diet. If you're serious about your diet you catch yourself and say, 'This is not what I want to do.'"

REHAB: TAKE TWO

In February 2007, Jacobs failed to meet Duffy prior to his Marc by Marc Jacobs show in London. After waiting a few hours, Duffy took a cab to the Dorchester Hotel and confronted Jacobs in his room. Duffy gave him until the day after their Louis Vuitton show—then he was taking him back to rehab.

At first, Jacobs tried to make a deal to buy himself another chance, another month. He said he would change on his own, but Duffy was adamant. He threatened to quit if Jacobs didn't agree to

The Marc Jacobs collection is often the can't-miss runway show of Mercedes-Benz Fashion Week. *Above*, a model showcases an outfit from Jacobs's Fall 2008 collection.

return to rehab. The designer finally gave in. Duffy made arrangements and accompanied Jacobs to an addiction treatment center in Arizona in March 2007; he later transferred to a rehabilitation center in Malibu, California.

Jacobs and Duffy agreed that they should be upfront with the media—and consequently, the public—about his decision to seek treatment a second time. Jacobs told the *London Times* in 2008:

Naomi Campbell: Supermodel, Super Friend

Sixteen-year-old Naomi Campbell was just getting her start in the modeling business when she met 23-year-old Marc Jacobs in 1986. She was at a fitting for Jacobs's first fashion show.

"I was relieved because everyone else made me afraid of them," she told *Harper's Bazaar*. "Calvin (Klein) didn't talk to me, neither did Oscar (de la Renta), and Marc was just a regular person. It was (model) Christy (Turlington) who told me I was going to like him." The friendship between Campbell and Jacobs has been a constant in the pair's tumultuous lives.

Campbell was born in May 22, 1970, in South London. Respecting the wishes of her mother, Valerie Campbell, she has never met her father, who left then-18-year-old Valerie two months after the birth of their daughter.

Discovered while shopping in London, Campbell signed with Elite Model Management and, in 1988, became the first black cover girl on French *Vogue*. Her early modeling work included campaigns for Ralph Lauren, Lee Jeans, Olympus, and Versace. She has starred in music videos for Michael Jackson, Aretha Franklin, and George Michael. In 1994, she published a novel and released an album, though neither was a commercial success.

While her good looks and style brought her fame, Campbell's anger—which she has blamed on drug dependency and the

There's an expression: "You're only as sick as your secrets." I tried to keep a lid on things when I was a kid, and that created a lot of problems. There is some kind of release in being honest and straightforward, not least because if you say it first that takes the sting out. Now I don't know how to behave any differently. Whether you can't work out the design of a strap on a shoulder bag or you're having a problem with alcohol, I always found that when I talked about it I could start to move on.

abandonment by her father—has brought her infamy. She has admitted to a seven-year drug dependency and checked into rehab in 1999.

In recent years, Campbell has faced a number of legal issues. In 2000, she pleaded guilty to assaulting her assistant with a telephone in her hotel room. In 2005, she allegedly slapped another assistant and hit her with a BlackBerry phone. Later that same year, Italian actress Yvonne Sciò claimed Campbell hit her at a Rome hotel, allegedly because Sciò was wearing the same dress as Campbell. In January 2007, Campbell pleaded guilty to a charge of assault against her housekeeper; she was sentenced to five days of community service and ordered to attend an anger management course.

In 2008, she was arrested at Heathrow Airport on suspicion of assaulting a police officer after her luggage was lost; she was sentenced to 200 hours of community service and has been banned from flying British Airways ever again. In March 2010, Campbell's limousine driver filed a complaint claiming the model slapped and punched him; that matter was dropped when the driver opted not to pursue criminal charges. Also in 2010, Campbell was summoned to testify in the war crimes trial against Charles Taylor, former president of Liberia, about a large, uncut "blood diamond" he allegedly gave her.

Campbell says her very public problems have forced her to face her own demons. "I had to look in the mirror and face mine and until I did there wasn't going to be a change in my life and I didn't want to be the way I was," she told CNN in 2010. "I think I've matured and I've grown up a lot. I've made my mistakes as the whole world knows, but today I feel good about myself."

Duffy and Jacobs were still deciding how best to make their announcement when the *New York Post*'s famed Page Six celebrity gossip column ran the story. Duffy confirmed the facts, but rather than calling the *Post* directly, he leaked the news to *Women's Wear Daily*, a publication he hoped would be kinder to Jacobs. The media strategy worked: the subsequent news stories were generally sympathetic and supportive. *New York Times* writer Amy Larocca, for example, reported on March 12, 2007:

> Marc Jacobs went into rehab today, his business partner Robert Duffy announced, and it's hard not to feel bad for him. He's struggled with addiction for years, and it's a relief to see that he's on top of the problem this time around. He pulled off fantastic shows in New York (Marc Jacobs), London (Marc by Marc Jacobs), and Paris (Louis Vuitton) last month, and is expected back the second week in April, which should give him plenty of time to get to work on the collections for the September shows. We'll be waiting for his next chapter.

Jacobs emerged from his second stint in rehab more energetic and focused than ever. He quickly returned to the work of designing and overseeing production of his Marc Jacobs, Marc by Marc Jacobs, and Louis Vuitton collections. "When he got sober, the spark came back, and that was amazing," Duffy told *Elle* in 2007. "That was everything."

The obsessions of Jacobs's past gave way to new, mostly healthy, obsessions. He became even more devoted to his fitness routine, spending two to three hours at the gym nearly every day. He gave up his bad habits—except smoking. It's a vice he clings to in spite of his otherwise healthy lifestyle.

"The gym to me is like in 'A Chorus Line.' It's the ballet," he told the *New Yorker* in 2008. "Everything is beautiful at the gym, everyone looks amazing. You just think it's like one big healthy circus going on out there: the bodies are great, people are jolly, and even when they're complaining about how strenuous it is,

In 2002, Jacob's hard work was celebrated with his induction into the Fashion Walk of Fame. Despite his healthy transformation and success, Jacobs continued to struggle with his drug and alcohol addiction and returned to rehab in 2007.

there's like, a kind of very good, positive we're-all-doing-something-good-for-ourselves. . . . And it's two and a half hours that I'm not smoking."

Although the objects of Jacobs's desires are healthier than they've been in the past, the designer continues to deal with an addictive personality. "Marc gets enchanted with certain things at certain times," Duffy told the *New Yorker* in 2008. "He was buying art until I was like, 'Marc, stop! You've got to pay your taxes!' I'm terrified of the day that he decides he wants to start gardening, because we'll have like Central Park in here or something."

Jacobs acknowledges his excesses but is more philosophical about them. "Anything that makes me feel good, I want to do more of," he told *Harper's Bazaar*. "Shopping, the gym, whatever.

The way fashion has gone today, I think the more you know about clothes, or the more you're taught about clothing in the classical sort of sense or in the school way of teaching, you become a little locked. It becomes harder to break the rules when you know them. . . . I have to say I think the best education for anybody—though it's very difficult to obtain—is to work. If there is a designer you admire, if there's any way to be around that working environment in any capacity, I think that would be far better training than going to school. I think that what I learned in Parsons is very valuable—patternmaking and things like that—but it does sort of get you locked into what you're taught.

—*Marc Jacobs on* The Charlie Rose Show, *1998*

I believe that you have to take chances. I never over-think whether people will love or hate something. I think that it's better to just get on with it.

—*Marc Jacobs in* Harper's Bazaar, *2009*

If you describe what I suffer from, it's wanting more of what makes me feel good. I don't know if that's so unusual. You know, I really believe my purpose in this world is to be happy, so I'm doing everything I can to keep it that way."

5

Everybody's
a Critic

Reading through these newspaper and magazine headlines, one would think designer Marc Jacobs could do no wrong:

"Fashion Report Card: Critics Love Jacobs, De la Renta, Herrera, DVF," *New York* magazine, February 2007

"Marc Jacobs: A Fashion Force to Be Reckoned With," *Independent*, May 2008

"Marc Jacobs Thrills Critics; Carolina Herrera 'Confounds,'" *New York* magazine, September 2009

"Critics Adore Marc Jacobs, Grapple with Rodarte's Boho Layers," *New York* magazine, February 2010

It is true that the long love affair between Jacobs and the fashion press has been largely sweet. But—like most relationships—it also has had its share of rocky patches.

Traditionally, fashion journalists produce copy for magazines, newspapers, and television. In recent years, fashion news and reviews have begun to be disseminated through Web sites and blogs. This means that not only do designers have more critics reviewing their work, but that criticism is being delivered more quickly and to a larger audience than ever before. Thanks to blogs and services like

Suzy Menkes, Fashion Critic

When a designer peeks out from behind the curtain and sees Suzy Menkes sitting in the front row at a fashion show, he or she is likely to feel two things simultaneously: fear and respect.

As fashion editor of the *International Herald Tribune*, Menkes's commentaries and critiques are read around the world. When she writes that a garment has graceful lines born of creative genius, readers of the fashion press take heed. When she disparages a collection, store buyers and fashionistas tend to run the other way. Fashion critics yield power, and Menkes's three decades of experience and global reach make her one of the most powerful.

Menkes was born in England in 1943. She spent a year in Paris studying dressmaking and then returned to Great Britain to study English and history at Cambridge University, where she became the first female editor of the university's newspaper. After graduation, Menkes landed a position as a junior fashion reporter for the *Times of London*. There, she met her future husband, David Spanier, the newspaper's political writer. They married in 1969 and had three sons; Spanier died in April 2000.

Menkes became the *Times*'s fashion editor in 1978. "Milan was just coming up, and the 1980s belonged to Italy, with the rise of Armani,

Twitter, critics are able to share commentary about a show's atmosphere or set even before the first model steps onto the stage, and followers can respond with their comments just as quickly.

The industry's most influential critic, Suzy Menkes of the *International Herald Tribune*, participated in a panel discussing the future of the fashion media during Berlin Fashion Week in January 2010. "The world changed when fashion, instead of being a monologue, became a conversation. And that's never going to stop," she told the audience.

Versace, and Gigli, and I covered all that," she told the *New Yorker* in 2001. In 1988, Menkes was hired as the head fashion reporter and editor for the *International Herald Tribune*. She is based in Paris, but she travels widely to cover her beat, often attending as many as 600 fashion shows each year. Her signature hairstyle is a flippy pompadour.

Menkes says she inherited her taste for luxury from her father. She loves fine fabrics and high fashion, but she admits there is one thing she's not crazy about: denim. "My weakness is I can't quite bring myself to really care about jeans," she told the *New Yorker* in 2001. "I've tried everything. Even when Dolce and Gabbana dress them up with all that embroidery and have Naomi's backside hanging out of them—to me, jeans are just jeans. There, I've admitted it. And, so long as I'm being absolutely honest, I don't really find sneakers so fascinating, either."

In addition to thousands of newspaper articles, Menkes has written three books: *The Royal Jewels, The Windsor Style,* and *Queen and Country.* She's also been a contributing writer to a handful of other books.

In 2005, the French government honored Menkes by naming her a chevalier of the Legion of Honor. A year later, she was named an officer of the Order of the British Empire for her services to journalism. Despite the honors, Menkes says she doesn't see herself as a fashion expert. "Journalists have to see themselves as what they are, a conduit between the creative people and the general public," she told the *San Francisco Chronicle* in 2010.

Fashion journalist Brandon Holley, who served as editor of *Jane*, a now-defunct young women's style magazine, said readers identify with bloggers' idiosyncratic and often rebellious voices. "Fashion moves so fast," Holley told the *New York Times* in 2005, "that readers find the blogs keep up better than even the tabloids like *Us Weekly*."

This changing world of fashion journalism means today's designers are subject to closer scrutiny than ever before. It's a fact Jacobs has learned firsthand.

TIMELINESS COUNTS

Runway shows don't begin on time. It is a fact. Fashion critics and Hollywood stars generally slip into their front-row seats 15 to 20 minutes late. They know the shows don't begin at their scheduled times, and designers know better than to start their shows without key audience members in place.

However, in the fall of 2007, Jacobs irked even the tardiest attendees when his New York Marc Jacobs show started two hours late. A few weeks later, his Paris Louis Vuitton show started at 8:45 P.M., one hour and 15 minutes past the invitation's scheduled start time. Rumors circulated that Jacobs had been drinking before the show, but the designer blamed his lateness on delays with earlier fashion shows, his need to take shower, and production difficulties.

The excuses didn't matter to members of the fashion press, who were overwhelmingly outraged by the delays. The two late shows might have been forgivable, but critics were unwilling to forgive what was becoming a habit of lateness: His Spring 2007 show was 70 minutes late because the clothes didn't arrive until 15 minutes after the show's scheduled start time. His Fall 2006 show was two hours late because his shoes were late arriving from Italy. His Fall 2004 show was almost two hours late. Shows for Spring 2004, Fall 2003, Fall 2002, and Spring 2001 all started more than an hour late.

In 2007, a large, disgruntled crowd of celebrities, journalists, and fashion industry's elite waited 75 minutes to see Jacobs's Spring 2008 collection (*above*). The designer who could do no wrong suddenly faced a barrage of criticism.

The 2007 shows—previewing his Spring 2008 collections—were simply the last straw for many critics. "Now, there's fashionably late and then there's just obnoxious," wrote critic Hadley Freeman in the *Guardian*.

Anna Wintour, editor in chief of American *Vogue*, was furious about the late start, telling the *Daily Telegraph*: "It's not as if he's some young 19-year-old. He's a grownup with a huge organization behind him."

The powerful Menkes weighed in on the issue with a September 12, 2007, review that began: "A bad, sad show from Marc Jacobs, running two hours late, high on hype and low on delivery, symbolized everything that is wrong with current fashion."

LASHING BACK

A month later, the *New York Post* reported that, while taking his bow on the catwalk at his Louis Vuitton show in Paris, Jacobs stuck out his tongue at Menkes. The newspaper went so far as to say the gesture was a direct response to Menkes's scathing review of Jacobs's Spring 2008 collection. Other critics suggested that Jacobs's onstage behavior was a sign of what must certainly be mental instability.

Jacobs's first reaction was to strike back at critics, telling them if they didn't like his behavior, they should skip his shows. He also threatened to move his Marc Jacobs shows to London or Paris, telling *Women's Wear Daily*: "I don't really feel a part of the American fashion community. I really feel like an outsider, I think we all do, and we feel unloved here, so we want to go somewhere else."

Jacobs didn't carry through on his threat and eventually went online to defend himself, writing the following in the comment section of *New York Times* writer Cathy Horyn's *On the Runway* blog:

> I did NOT stick my tongue out at Suzy Menkes. . . . I pulled a stupid face with my tongue out in happiness for being done with what has been a great but most stressful season for me. I am not stupid, childish or a vindictive person. . . . I had prior to the show left a silly t-shirt and a nice note for Suzy on her seat. Why would I do anything to further upset her? Right after a show!!?? . . . I am surprised that anyone who knows me at all thinks that I am that petty or stupid! Anyone who has ever been on a stage would know you can't actually see the audience. I made a face at no one in particular. . . . I didn't have a clue as to who was sitting there. Come on guys, give me a break!!!!

The litany of media attacks continued and reached beyond his designs and tardiness to touch on his appearance, his love life, and rumors of plastic surgery. "I'm starting to get very paranoid as to why it feels like so many people are against me, personally, at this point," Jacobs told the *New York Times* in 2007. "Despite whatever rumors you may have heard, I'm not out of my mind." The spat between Jacobs, Menkes, and the world's fashion critics was carried out in newspapers, magazines, and online for several weeks. Eventually, the issues were resolved or, at least, stopped making headlines.

Then, in February 2008, he began his Marc Jacobs show at New York's Lexington Armory just 20 minutes after its stated start time. His unexpected promptness (at least by fashion's standards) caught guests by surprise. As the band Sonic Youth performed and models paraded down the runway, attendees—

Jacobs, who draws his inspiration from old issues of fashion magazines, often blends looks from different decades together with a modern twist. In his September 2007 Fashion Week presentation (*above*) he combined elements from the 1950s with bright, striking colors that evoked the 1980s.

including editors Nina Garcia and Fabien Baron—were still struggling to find their seats. Stylist Rachel Zoe was so late, she was shut out completely.

The almost-on-time start earned a few mentions by critics who were beginning to understand that the only predictable thing about Jacobs was his unpredictability. But Jacobs's relationship with time could hardly continue to be the story—especially when he was doing what they'd asked by being prompt—so critics instead turned their attention to his collections. British *Vogue* was impressed with Jacobs's blend of 1980s new wave and 1950s beatnik stylings, writing: "We were struck by how fresh and energetic the collection felt, despite the vintage references." *Women's Wear Daily* called the collection "punk with ample parts pretty," while *Fashion Week Daily* called the show "a fun, exuberant extravaganza."

Finally, he was back in the headlines for his work instead of his behavior. In the years since, critics have loved certain Jacobs collections or at least aspects of them. The shoes in his Fall 2010 show in New York, for example, won raves. So did his Fall 2009 show, which the *Los Angeles Times* deemed "one of Jacobs' most saleable collections in years, with lots of separates to buy," and which *Women's Wear Daily* saluted as a "masterfully audacious collection."

Of course, there have been plenty of misses along the way as well. His Fall 2005 collection was disparaged by many fashion critics as too dark and too funky. His Spring 2007 collection for Louis Vuitton was labeled "unremarkable," and critics speculated that retailers would have a difficult time selling the 1930s-inspired tunic in his 2008 Marc Jacobs Ready to Wear collection.

Jacobs is realistic enough to know that critics are not going to like everything he designs and produces. If critics did nothing but applaud his work, consumers would stop reading their reviews, assuming they had become a rubber stamp for anything he put his name on. What he fears more than bad press is no press at all.

No designer, not even Jacobs, can create a successful collection every year. His Fall 2005 presentation (*above*) was considered too dark, while other disappointing shows featured designs that did not appeal to retailers.

ELEMENTS OF STYLE

I'd like to believe that the women who wear my clothes are not dressing for other people, that they're wearing what they like and what suits them. It's not a status thing.

—*Marc Jacobs in* Index *magazine, 2001*

My greatest hero in fashion will always be [Yves] Saint Laurent, (but) I do think Ralph Lauren is the greatest American designer. . . . I just think that (he) creates his world and a vision—and that vision is so complete. That voice is so clear. Everything within that world is that particular singular vision. On that level, Ralph Lauren really is the ultimate American designer. I don't think we've ever had this master plan or master vision in the way Ralph Lauren has. We are very impulsive. We do what we like and the people in our company are the same. Ralph has created a world that people aspire to and I don't think it's what we're all about at all. We create things, whether they're T-shirts or little key chains, (and they're) us because we've done (them), but it's not an aspirational sort of thing.

—*Marc Jacobs in* Women's Wear Daily, *2010*

"In the most basic way I can say it," he told the *New York Times* in 2007, "coming from a psychological place, what I love more than anything is attention. That is about as honest of a statement that I could possibly make. I want a reaction, because I want attention."

And reactions are just what the critics will continue to provide.

6

The Many Faces
of Marc Jacobs

Night vs. day. Polished vs. pretty. Bold vs. bashful. In Marc Jacobs's mind, that's how distinctly different his Marc Jacobs and Louis Vuitton women's collections are. And each of those collections is designed with a very different woman in mind.

Jacobs sees the Marc Jacobs woman as someone who is gentle and introverted. The look is soft, poetic, and romantic. He takes much of his influence for the Marc Jacobs line from his personal perceptions of New York, tending toward styles that are logical and credible.

The Vuitton woman, on the other hand, oozes confidence and seeks attention. Jacobs allows Paris to influence his Louis Vuitton designs, which he says are about suspending logic and flaunting all that you have.

Collaboration is a common link between the Marc Jacobs and Louis Vuitton lines. Jacobs stresses that he works with talented and passionate designers on both brands and that the end result is not the manifestation of his singular vision, but the collective vision of each member of the creative team.

"At Vuitton, I have to define what Vuitton is as a bag (and) as a woman," he told *Women's Wear Daily* in 2010. "And people carry Vuitton luggage and when I looked at that, I thought,

LV: The Early Years

When he opened his first store in Paris in 1854, luggage maker Louis Vuitton couldn't possibly have imagined that his little company would one day become the world's leading luxury brand.

Vuitton got his start by designing the first flat-topped trunks that were lightweight and airtight. At the time, most trunks had rounded tops for water to run off. Vuitton's trunks were immediate hits because they could easily be stacked in railway cars, unlike trunks with rounded tops. Vuitton also created trunks large enough to accommodate the ample crinolines worn by France's Empress Eugenie, wife of Napoleon III. This early meeting of the needs of royalty can be considered the beginning of Vuitton's carefully crafted image as a brand of luxury and celebrity.

Interest in travel was growing in the mid-nineteenth century, and Louis Vuitton began to make its mark as one of the first luggage companies prepared to meet the needs of wealthy vacationers and adventure-seekers. The company quickly became known for its designer luggage pattern: a beige-on-brown monogram, *LV*. Vuitton's high-quality traveling trunks were such a hit that he had to expand his factory within a few years, relocating in 1860 to Asnières, a northwest suburb of Paris. As the years went by, the Vuitton line gained international recognition and admiration, thanks in part to medals it won at the 1867 and 1889 World's Fairs, both held in Paris.

it's not because (the luggage) is the most practical or lightest weight—it's the most identifiable. So, it's about somebody wanting to be recognized. . . . It's about this woman (who's) got the latest bag, she's busting out of the corset. She wants to be seen and noticed. She's more superficial—and I don't mean that in a negative way. I think that's glorious that somebody wants to show off like that. But that's not what our clothes are about at Marc Jacobs."

When Louis died in 1892, his son, Georges, took over leadership of the company. He is credited with developing what is recognized as the first "designer label" on a product. Georges is thought to have created more than 700 new Vuitton designs, including the "Steamer" bag, a predecessor to the soft-sided luggage most travelers use today. The Steamer was originally intended to be used as a laundry bag that would fit inside a travel trunk, but it gained popularity for its own merits.

Georges Vuitton died in 1936; his son Gaston-Louis Vuitton then took over the company and continued to lead it forward. Designs were revamped and processes were enhanced to ensure customers received the highest-quality products possible. For instance, in the late 1950s, the company was able to perfect a method of coating that allowed the fabric beneath to remain soft, flexible, and beautiful, while adding strength and protection from the elements; it's a coating that is still used today in the making of some of Vuitton's handbags and wallets.

In 1987, Moët et Chandon and Hennessy merged with Louis Vuitton to form the world's largest luxury goods conglomerate, LVMH. Today, the LVMH group includes more than 50 luxury brands, including perfumes, cosmetics, jewelry, watches, fashion, leather goods, and Moët et Chandon champagne.

Louis Vuitton is so beloved that the Louis Vuitton Museum in Asnières celebrates the brand. Privately arranged tours of the museum and its exhibits—connected to the only production facility for Louis Vuitton from 1959 to 1977—allow visitors to pay tribute to the company's many outstanding creations.

At Vuitton, design is a matter of balance. Jacobs must always keep one foot firmly rooted in the past while marching steadily toward the future. The designer saves his most ornate and elaborate flourishes for the collections at Louis Vuitton. Hand beading, fine fabrics, and the iconic logo combine for fashions that cost as much as $10,000 for a single gown. "Louis Vuitton is a unique organization: the products never go on sale, nor are they sold at duty-free shops," he told the *Telegraph* in 2010. "We create what people desire. And I love that commitment to quality."

At Marc Jacobs, the designer creates fashions for men, women, and children—the women's collection being most popular. While generally more understated than his Louis Vuitton collection, the Marc Jacobs line is not for wallflowers or those on a tight fashion budget. Handbags by Marc Jacobs, for example, sell for $500 to $1,500; a double-breasted tailored wool women's coat from his Fall/Winter 2010 collection retails for $2,000; and a pleated skirt in acetate and rayon sells for $700. Over the years, the Marc Jacobs collection has grown to include fragrance, a home collection—including crystal, sterling silver, cashmere pillows, and other luxury accessories—and eyewear.

Regardless of the collection, Jacobs's designs are admired and in high demand. It's become routine for competing fashion brands (even mass marketers like Old Navy and Abercrombie & Fitch) to imitate his designs, and counterfeiters produce and market copies of his handbags and accessories.

"I like the fact that each season there is a challenge, well, two challenges," he told the *Telegraph*. "I wear the same clothes, but I think differently. I have different 'heads' for different teams. I very much go with the environment. In New York (when I'm designing Marc Jacobs), I'm very sensitive to my experiences and my friends—it's more personal. In Paris, when it's Louis Vuitton, the look is much more extrovert, for a luxury-hungry show-off."

The international clout and appeal of Louis Vuitton has given Jacobs the opportunity to quickly expand his business in other countries. Marc Jacobs boutiques have opened in major cities all over the world, including in Dubai (*above*).

JACOBS FOR MEN, KIDS, BARGAIN HUNTERS

While Marc Jacobs and Louis Vuitton are the designer's most talked-about collections, he is also the creative mind behind three additional lines: Marc Jacobs Menswear, Marc by Marc Jacobs, and Little Marc Jacobs.

Marc Jacobs Menswear got its start in 1994. Jacobs, who himself often wears a kilt rather than trousers, has gained a reputation for designing men's clothing that is both comfortable and luxurious. Popular styles in recent collections have included zip-up hoodies, faded jeans, and boldly colored dress shirts. He has created blazers, two-tone T-shirts, leather biker-inspired jackets, and blousey linen shirts adorned with whimsical motifs. In June 2002, Marc Jacobs Menswear beat out Ralph Lauren and Sean John for the Council

In addition to the Marc Jacobs collection and Louis Vuitton, Jacobs also designs menswear, clothes for children, and the moderately priced Marc by Marc Jacobs. *Above*, a model presents an outfit from the Marc by Marc Jacobs line.

of Fashion Designers of America's Menswear Designer of the Year award. Even after accepting the honor, Jacobs told the *Daily News Record*, "I still don't think of myself as a men's wear designer," adding that making clothing for women "is what I really love."

Trendy Marc Jacobs shoppers are, of course, eager to dress their offspring in designer clothing, so Jacobs launched a children's collection, Little Marc by Marc Jacobs, in the spring of 2007. "So many of our friends started having babies, and they asked us for thermal cashmere sweaters for their kids," Robert Duffy told *Time* magazine in 2008. "We started making a few items and selling them in our stores."

The items became so popular that Jacobs signed a licensing deal with French children's wear manufacturer Zannier Group. They've since launched a full line of chic clothes for kids ages newborn to 12 that include hoodie sweatshirts, graphic T-shirts, jeans, and sweaters.

Even the tiniest designer clothes come with designer-size price tags. Some Little Marc cashmere sweaters, for example, retail for nearly $400, while light-wash denim jeans sell for $95, and embellished ballet flats retail for $240.

Additionally, the designer has a diffusion line called Marc by Marc Jacobs, which first hit the runway in 2001. The Marc by Marc Jacobs collection includes many of the designer's vintage lines, feminine details, and oversized buttons, but it creates those looks using less expensive materials. A cashmere Marc Jacobs sweater, for instance, might sell for $600, while the same design in a less lavish fiber might retail for $160 through Marc by Marc Jacobs.

"There is a huge difference in feel and quality, but there is a customer for both," Duffy told *Fortune* magazine in 2007. At Marc by Marc Jacobs and Little Marc, 70 percent of sales are what Duffy refers to as "junk." Customers are buying up $20 T-shirts, fragrances, diaper totes, and costume jewelry.

Alexandra Shulman, editor of British *Vogue*, says the multiple lines of clothing and their combined popularity mean that Jacobs's

ELEMENTS OF STYLE

I was really ambitious and sort of passionate about what I'm doing now since I was a very young age. I guess that was really lucky in a way. I had this real desire to be in fashion and work in fashion, so I stayed very, very focused. My experience has sort of [taught] me that if you stay focused and you stay passionate, then you can do anything.

—*Marc Jacobs on* The Charlie Rose Show/Charlie's Green Room, *2008*

A trend that makes me cringe? There isn't one. I don't believe in good and bad taste.

—*Marc Jacobs in* InStyle *magazine, 2009*

Getting dressed should be an emotional thing.

—*Marc Jacobs in* InStyle *magazine, 2010*

I don't like things that are obvious. Just beauty by itself is too obvious. I love imperfection.

—*Marc Jacobs in the* New York Times, *2010*

influence on fashion is significant. "Marc is one (of) the great contemporary fashion talents," she told the *Guardian* in 2008. "He has pitch-perfect style which he can translate into a handbag range for Vuitton or T-shirts for his Marc line. He seems to be able to pin down cool again and again without being alienating."

Elle magazine editor in chief Lorraine Candy agrees that Jacobs has wide-reaching appeal and notes that even his least expensive offerings are important because they allow customers to have a representation of his designs, regardless of their checking account balance. "He's democratizing fashion in a way, by making the Marc Jacobs brand completedly accessible," she told the *Observer* in 2008.

7

Famous Fans

Celebrities such as director Sofia Coppola and actress Hilary Swank have been known to dress in head-to-toe Marc Jacobs attire. Cameron Diaz routinely carries a Marc Jacobs tote. Model Kate Moss and singer Gwen Stefani wear his dresses.

The front row of his runway shows have included the likes of entertainer-turned-designer Victoria Beckham, models Naomi Campbell and Sophie Dahl, rocker Debbie Harry, French actress Catherine Deneuve, and Swiss tennis star Roger Federer. While other designers sometimes pay A-list celebrities to attend their shows, Jacobs's shows attract famous folks who actually choose to be there.

With his many lines and varied price points, Jacobs has designs to suit nearly every man and woman. It is just that some of his most devoted fans happen to star in blockbuster movies, front their own rock bands, and win major sporting events. These famous fans wear Louis Vuitton or Marc Jacobs or even Marc by Marc Jacobs fashions when they do interviews or appear on talk shows—without even being asked to do so.

"We—we meaning myself, Robert Duffy and anybody who is involved in any (public relations) capacity—have never courted celebrity," Jacobs told *Women's Wear Daily* in 2004. "And I'm kind of proud of that, that we're not like salesmen and we're not kind of out there and sort of saying wear this, do this, promote us." That's not to say Jacobs doesn't appreciate his most prominent clients.

Fans of Jacobs's work include director Sofia Coppola, actress Winona Ryder, and recording artist Kanye West. The front rows of his fashion shows are often a mix of industry leaders and celebrities like model-actress Milla Jovovich (*above,* in white).

In fact, the designer has teamed up with his famous fans—and friends—on more than one occasion to star in both Louis Vuitton and Marc Jacobs ad campaigns.

His 2008 Vuitton campaign, for instance, featured photos of director Francis Ford Coppola and his daughter Sofia standing in a field with a monogrammed tote. There is another with Keith Richards of the Rolling Stones playing his guitar in a hotel room next to a custom-made instrument case. In a third, former Soviet leader Mikhail Gorbachev sits with a Vuitton satchel in the back seat of a limousine near a remnant of the Berlin Wall. And the list goes on.

When Marc Jacobs found himself in a meeting in the fall of 2008 to brainstorm an upcoming advertising campaign for Louis Vuitton, he was struck with inspiration. "I just blurted out: 'I think we should do Madonna,'" the designer told *Women's Wear Daily* in 2008. Jacobs had been to a concert by the Material Girl in Paris the night before. "I was totally just blown away by it, and moved by her performance, by what she had to say, and her energy," he said.

The meeting wasn't even over when Jacobs sent a text message to Madonna, asking if the pop icon might be interested. Within about five minutes, she sent back her reply: "I'd love to." The recording star's devotion to Louis Vuitton and designer Jacobs predates her stint as featured model. Madonna often opts for Vuitton or Jacobs attire when she makes appearances and is a frequent attendee of the designer's runway shows, both in New York and Europe.

The Jacobs-Madonna collaboration resulted in a series of images, shot by photographer Steven Meisel and art directed by Jacobs, that portray Madonna as a smoldering sex symbol in a Parisian-themed cafe. The photos were featured in advertisements for Louis Vuitton's Spring/Summer 2009 collection. "I wanted the campaign to be very bold, very sensual and very atmospheric," Jacobs told the *New Straits Times* in 2008. "To carry off all these references and all this sophistication, we needed the ultimate performer, and for me, that was Madonna."

The campaign was so well-received that Jacobs and Madonna teamed up again for Vuitton's Fall/Winter 2009 collection. In the photos, also shot by Meisel, Madonna wears short, poufy silk skirts, fingerless gloves, and thigh-high boots. She also wears bunny-ear headbands, inspired by a headpiece she wore to the Costume Institute Gala at New York's Metropolitan Museum in May 2009. Madonna attended the Costume Institute celebration with Jacobs.

Another Jacobs ad campaign that gathered considerable press saw the designer team up with his pal, former Spice Girl Victoria Beckham. The campaign's first image, which broke in the February 2008 issue of *W* magazine, showed a giant Marc Jacobs shopping bag with Beckham's legs peeking out, but no signs of her very famous face. "There was a lot of discussion about Victoria being in our ads and tons of blogs on the Internet about 'Should she or shouldn't she?', 'What's going on with Marc Jacobs?', and 'Has he lost his mind?'" Jacobs told *Women's Wear Daily* in 2008. "We thought the funniest thing would be to show the Victoria Beckham ads that don't show Victoria Beckham, but just to see those legs coming out of the bag."

While some critics thought the ads poked fun at Beckham, she defended them in a 2008 interview with *W*: "The images are humorous and ironic. You can't be afraid to experiment with fashion, especially when working with Marc and Juergen Teller—you have to push the envelope and show a different side. Marc is a genius. I completely trusted his vision and the opportunity to work with Juergen again after so many years was a privilege."

Jacobs's celebrity connections go on and on. Actress Uma Thurman posed for a line of seductive Louis Vuitton ads. So have actresses Jennifer Lopez, Scarlett Johansson, Chloë Sevigny, and Christina Ricci, and supermodel Gisele Bündchen. Actor Hayden Christensen and hip-hop musician Pharrell have both appeared as models for the Louis Vuitton's luggage and ready-to-wear lines.

 Fashion icon Madonna happily participated in Louis Vuitton's Fall/Winter 2009 ad campaign. She promoted Jacobs's designs at the Metropolitan Museum's annual Costume Institute Gala in 2009.

Even when they're not officially featured in advertising campaigns, celebrities seem to be doing their part to promote Jacobs's designs. Vuitton bags and purses have a lengthy list of superstar fans who proudly display their "Monogram canvas" items. Celebrities such as Lindsay Lohan, Paris and Nicky Hilton, Nicole Richie, and Angelina Jolie are often seen and photographed with their favorite Vuitton accessories.

While these celebrity connections may seem like no big deal, their reverberations can be felt around the world. When the perfect style is worn by the right person, it can be a powerful marketing tool—for designers and retailers alike.

WHY CELEBRITIES MATTER

The fact that Jacobs has so many famous fans has become even more important in recent years. That's because shoppers 35 years old and younger are more likely than ever to cite celebrities as an important source of new fashion ideas. If celebrity influence on everyday fashion weren't so prevalent, magazines wouldn't devote pages to features telling readers where they can purchase a necklace seen on a favorite television show or the swimsuit a popular actress was photographed wearing while on vacation.

That influence over Americans' shopping habits was verified in a 2008 survey conducted by Cotton Incorporated Lifestyle Monitor, a North Carolina–based research and promotional organization. The poll gathered information from 4,000 shoppers ages 16 to 70. Among all women surveyed, 60 percent cite fashion magazines, TV shows, and celebrities as their top sources for clothing ideas. If it looks good on Julia Roberts, they reason, it may look good on me. Or, if I dress the same way as my superstar idol, perhaps I'll look as beautiful as she does.

If that percentage seems exaggerated, consider the fashion influence of First Lady Michelle Obama. Sure, her agenda has included reaching out to military families and addressing the issue of childhood obesity, but it is her sense of style that grabbed the most headlines. From her belted cardigans to bold jewelry and sleeve-less sheath dresses, Michelle Obama's tastes and style have influenced millions of women. When she danced with the president at his inauguration ball in January 2009 wearing a white chiffon, one-shoulder gown covered in fluffy appliqués and beading, she gave its designer, then-26-year-old Jason Wu, a career boost like no other.

Prior to his brush with political power, Wu was selling his clothes in 10 stores and employed six people. According to a September 2009 report in the *Wall Street Journal*, Wu's 2008 revenues were

ELEMENTS OF STYLE

The days of the designer in his ivory tower inventing a "look" that he dictates is fashion are over. That whole old-school narrative of "I just took a trip to India, and the colors and the spices and the sky and the seashells on the beaches inspired my new collection" is kind of ridiculous.

—Marc Jacobs in the New York Times, *2002*

I use the word "classic" to describe anything that feels familiar in a way. Classic to me is something that's endured. Now it may have only endured in my head, but it has endured, you know what I mean? Like I say like, "Oh, you know those classic square-toe shoes." Well … (laughter). Well, I think that just says it all right there.

—Marc Jacobs in Women's Wear Daily, *2004*

I don't like it when people are precious about clothes. My ultimate vision of a contemporary woman is someone like (British model) Stella Tennant, who will show up in a beautiful couture ballgown by Galliano and throw a Levi's jean jacket over it.

—Marc Jacobs in the Evening Standard, *2005*

$800,000. Within nine months of Mrs. Obama wearing his gown, Wu's designs were being sold in 40 stores, including Saks, Neiman Marcus, Harrods in London, Lane Crawford in China, and Harvey Nichols in England. Gustavo Rangel, Wu's chief financial officer, said the company was on track to make $4 million in 2009.

With the power of celebrity so widely known, Jacobs took the fashion world by surprise in February 2010 when he announced

Picture This: Juergen Teller

Juergen Teller has been one of Marc Jacobs's closest collaborators since 1998—yet his name is unknown to most fashionistas. That's because he's not a model. He's not a designer. He doesn't have a fashion TV show or blog or Web site.

Teller is the guy behind the camera lens. He shoots the photos that show up in Jacobs's often outlandish advertising campaigns: Victoria Beckham in a giant shopping bag, Sofia Coppola peeking out from under a bed sheet, Dakota Fanning in child-size versions of grown-up gowns.

Teller, who was born in Germany, didn't grow up dreaming of becoming a photographer. He told *Index* magazine in 2000:

> I started off making bows for violins. My dad's whole family, my grandfather, my great-grandfather, all did bridges for violins. My dad used to play five instruments. It's normally a three-year apprenticeship to be a bow maker. But I developed an allergy to the wood and I got really heavy asthma. So the doctor sent me for an air change, and I went off with my cousin Helmut, who was already a photographer. That's when I got into taking pictures. And because the social system in Germany is so good, and it wasn't my fault that I couldn't be a bow maker, they sent me to school for photography.

he was no longer inviting stars to sit in the front row at his runway shows. His reasoning: They distract the audience. Jacobs told Style.com in 2010:

> Last season, we had two celebrities, one because Lady Gaga was doing our party, and she didn't even make it to her seat because we started the show before she got there. And one was Madonna. She came backstage, and I was like, "What do you

When he was in his early twenties, Teller moved to London, where he started taking photos of musicians and published his work in the magazines *Face* and *i-D*. He's since become one of the world's most influential contemporary fashion photographers, having shot major ad campaigns for Comme des Garçons, Stüssy, and Helmut Lang.

Teller and Jacobs met through Teller's ex-wife, fashion stylist Venetia Scott. They became fast friends, and soon they began working together on an ad with vocalist Kim Gordon from the American rock band Sonic Youth. They've since gained a reputation for casting the most unpredictable individuals in their ads: indie rock musician Stephen Malkmus, artist and photographer Cindy Sherman, actress Winona Ryder—just after she wore a Marc Jacobs dress to her 2002 shoplifting trial. Teller, himself, has even shown up in Jacobs's photo-based advertising campaigns.

"It's basically people we know or admire," Teller told the *New York Times Magazine* in 2009. "As friends, we talk about films and shows we've seen. Or someone will mention that they just had dinner with Cindy Sherman and then one of us will be, "Why not use her for a campaign?' That's basically how it happens."

Teller takes pride in the fact that his photos are absolutely never retouched. "I'm interested in the person I photograph," he told the *New York Times Magazine* in 2008. "The world is so beautiful as it is, there's so much going on which is sort of interesting. It's just so crazy, so why do I have to put some retouching on it. It's just pointless to me."

In addition to his commercial work, Teller shoots for *W* magazine and presents his work in museums and galleries. A coffee table book of his advertising photos, *Juergen Teller: Marc Jacobs Advertising*, was released in 2009.

Jacobs receives the Council of Fashion Designers of America award for International Designer of the Year, his ninth award from the organization. His hard work has influenced people around the world through fashion magazines, celebrities, televisions shows, and film.

do with her now?" Because it's not like she was invited. She just called and said she was coming, and we weren't holding the show for her. She just came, and that was it. There are certain things I can't control.

We used to have all the celebrities and people there, and I think that at that moment in time, that's what people loved. It generated so much press and at a certain point it was like, "Did anybody actually watch the show?"

Jacobs, a celebrity who attracts a good share of paparazzi himself, is unapologetic about his new decision to exclude stars from his shows. He wants critics and buyers to focus on the clothes. He also wants to be sure his approach to fashion remains honest and straightforward. "My influences and inspirations are always pretty much . . . consistent, I think," he told the *Evening Standard* in 2001. "You know—music and friends and so on." And he said nothing about those friends being famous.

8

Finding His Place
in Fashion History

When *Time* magazine issued its 2010 list of the 100 Most Influential People in the World, designer Marc Jacobs found himself in some pretty powerful company. He was the only fashion designer named to a list that included world leaders (U.S. president Barack Obama, Japanese prime minister Yukio Hatoyama), athletes (golfer Phil Mickelson, tennis star Serena Williams), musicians (Elton John, Lady Gaga), and actors (Neil Patrick Harris, Robert Pattinson).

The list is an annual who's who in the world. When the magazine asked Jacobs's pal Victoria Beckham to pay tribute to him, she wrote this:

Marc Jacobs is undoubtedly one of the most influential designers of all time. He has never followed fashion or trends; he follows his heart and sets trends. His passion for popular culture infuses his designs with irreverence, color and energy. It's what sets him far ahead of his peers. He is not afraid to go against the grain and never feels the pressure to conform.

Marc, 47, is one of the most interesting and intellectual men I have ever known. He inspires and educates me every time we meet. He changes how we see fashion with each collection he shows, be it his work for Louis Vuitton or his own baby, the Marc Jacobs line, which he started in 1986. He finds beauty all around him, and his aesthetic is like no other. You can always tell when someone is wearing Marc Jacobs.

Without debate, Jacobs is one of the most popular, profitable, and prolific designers working today. At Louis Vuitton, he is responsible for designing more than a billion dollars worth of clothing and accessories for men and women. Between Vuitton, Marc Jacobs, and Marc by Marc Jacobs, he oversees eight runway shows in New York and Paris each year, plus advertising, fragrances, housewares, jewelry, boutiques, a Web site, media interviews, and so much more. The New Yorker's influence is felt at every level and every price point of fashion.

But the question is, what kind of long-term influence will this currently red-hot designer have? Is Jacobs in the league of great designers before him: Gianni Versace, Coco Chanel, Calvin Klein? Is his the sort of creative mind that will be revered long after he's sketched his last sketch and pinned his last pattern?

Cathy Horyn, fashion critic for the *New York Times*, seems to think so. She counts his collections among fashion's great treasures, writing in 2007: "At some point in the next 20 to 30 years, an astute collector of Marc Jacobs's clothing will be sitting on a gold mine of information. Distance is required to appreciate the designs he has done for Louis Vuitton and his own label— the randomness, the appropriations, the superficial strafing of culture."

Horyn is not alone in her praise. Amy Spindler of the *New York Times* wrote about Jacobs in 1997: "He has become the most consistently strong, individualistic, real, live, kicking designer in New York." When Parsons School of Design honored Jacobs in 2004, design department chair Tim Gunn called him "a visionary force in the fashion industry."

Aaron Hicklin, writing in *Out* magazine in 2007, said: "For someone in an industry as notoriously fickle as fashion, Marc Jacobs has remarkable staying power—not that he's ever likely to take his success for granted. His legendary work ethic ('rebel without a pause' was how one publication characterized him) has taken him to heights unmatched by any American designer, but his response to each success is to work even harder to sustain it the next time."

Still, after the tributes and awards and billions of dollars in sales, Jacobs finds it difficult to accept that he's "influential." In a 2004 article in *Women's Wear Daily*, Jacobs said: "It's such a difficult thing to say I'm an influential designer. I didn't decide to be influential. I just make things I like." He may not have set out to make an enduring mark on the annals of fashion, but after creating cutting-edge fashion year after year for more than 20 years, it is clear that he has.

Jacobs's broad appeal and keen sense of "what's next?" has made him the fashion industry's golden boy. In 2001, actress Winona Ryder was arrested for shoplifting an armful of his cashmere tops from a Los Angeles department store; Jacobs responded by giving her a starring role in one of his ad campaigns. In 2010, Jacobs, himself, stripped naked to pose with a strategically placed bottle of perfume for another ad campaign. A quirky, keen sense of humor is also part of his appeal.

Wendy Dagworthy, head of the school of fashion and textiles at London's Royal College of Art, says Jacobs could be the next Yves Saint Laurent. "There's that classic look to his designs," she

Although he is relatively young, Jacobs is considered one of the world's greatest designers, joining the ranks of Coco Chanel and Gianni Versace. His shows are highly anticipated events around the world, including Beijing, China (*above*).

told the *Observer* in 2008. "But he's a real original and it's these sorts of people who push the future of fashion. These are the people who are remembered."

JACOBS'S DESIGN HALL OF FAME

Some of the specific innovations he'll be remembered for aren't really innovations at all, but rather reincarnations. Jacobs has always turned to the past for inspiration. Some of his favorites are the 1950s prom dress and the Peter Pan collar of the 1960s; both have been reimagined for multiple appearances on his runway.

Law and Order

Think fashion designers, with their supermodel friends and fancy runway shows, are exempt from legal troubles? Think again.

The fashion industry is subject to a wide array of laws and legal issues, ranging from U.S. and international copyright, trademark law, trade dress, design and utility patents, trade secrets, licensing, and counterfeiting. Additionally, designers have to be concerned with laws affecting commercial operating agreements, business structures, employment issues, marketing, advertising and promotion, customs issues, and more. In fact, there are so many fashion-specific legal concerns that some attorneys and law firms actually specialize in "fashion law."

Designer Marc Jacobs has seen his share of legal troubles over the years. Sometimes he was the one being sued; other times he was the one doing the suing. In 2006, for example, Jacobs was among eight makers of luxury items—including Burberry and Givenchy—that sued a trust that leased retail space in New York's Chinatown. The companies claimed counterfeit purses, watches, scarves, and other goods were being sold from the shops. Related undercover policing resulted in the closure of 32 shops and the confiscation of more than $1 million worth of counterfeit goods.

In early 2008, Jacobs was accused of plagiarism. Göran Olofsson accused Jacobs of copying a scarf created in the 1950s by his father, Swedish designer Gösta Olofsson. In March of that same year,

The layers that were so prevalent in his 1992 grunge-inspired collection have endured through the years.

The waffle-weave fabric most often associated with long johns is hip thanks to the update Jacobs gave it in 1997. Introduced in cashmere and an assortment of colors, the weave has become a Jacobs signature.

Jacobs reached a cash settlement with the family; the issue never went to trial.

In November 2008, the Marc Jacobs fashion company paid $1 million to settle allegations that it bribed the superintendent of New York City's Twenty-sixth Street Armory to use the location for its signature fashion shows. The armory's superintendent, James Jackson, pleaded guilty to accepting bribes from Jacobs and other companies to hold certain dates for events, simplify their paperwork, and allow early access to the building for setup. Jacobs had an exclusive arrangement with the armory, one of the few spaces in the city that is large enough to hold thousands of people with unobstructed views, during Fashion Week.

In February 2010, Jacobs's company sued designer Christian Audigier's Nervous Tattoo Inc. for trade dress and trademark infringement over purse designs. The bags in question, from Jacobs's Pretty Nylon Tote collection and Audigier's Ed Hardy Jana collection, had similar bucket shapes, tied handles, and quilted logos.

Other designers have battled allegations of discrimination or sued distributors for breach of contract. In 1998, Ralph Lauren, the man who made polo shirts chic, even filed a lawsuit against the official magazine of the U.S. Polo Association for allegedly violating his copyright of the word *polo*.

Jeannie Suk, a Guggenheim fellow at Harvard Law School, is one of the nation's experts on American fashion designers and their need for copyright protection. "People have a lifelong relationship with the clothes that they put on themselves," she told the *Boston Globe* in 2010. "One way or another, we all have a stake in what we wear. When you learn the way that the law regulates that part of your life, you start to ask questions. No matter what kind of clothes you wear."

Of course, Jacobs's handbags—for Louis Vuitton or his own label—have an almost cult-like following. There are canvas doctor's-style bags trimmed with ostrich-skin handles, quilted bags with antique-style heavy brass chain trim, glossy patent leather clutches, padlocked bags, crocodile bags, embroidered bags, and more.

"The handbag increasingly occupies a curious place in the hierarchy of fashion, at once kingpin and jokester," critic Cathy Horyn wrote in the *New York Times* in 2007. "It drives sales and elicits contempt from those who believe it is responsible for a creative dumbing-down within the fashion industry. Nonetheless, as a visual form, the handbag keeps evolving and surprising us, and Mr. Jacobs has done more to influence that than anyone else."

Staying on the top rung of the fashion ladder—without becoming stale or predictable—has taken hard work by both Jacobs and his business partner, Robert Duffy. He credits his continued youthful appeal to his ability to successfully partner with young artists and designers. "I do have quite young taste," he told *Women's Wear Daily* in 2004. "I love young things. I think youth and energy are just the most beautiful things in the world. I don't know anybody who wants to look old. So I mean I'm attracted to young things and I do get inspired by young things or fresh things. And, even when I'm doing something that's ironically dowdy, it's because it seems to be what appeals to young people at the moment."

Jacobs says his longevity in the business is due to staying relevant, understanding his customer, and his never-say-die determination. "When you're passionate about something, you just don't quit," he told the *Evening Standard* in 2001. "I've been in and out of business and I've had jobs which I was fired from—and every single time I thought my life was over and I'd never work in fashion again. And you know what? As long as I was passionate, I found work. And each time it was better and better."

Buzz about Jacobs's career ambitions have been circulating around the industry and in the media for nearly a decade.

With his considerable talent and strong sense of style, Marc Jacobs has created a fashion empire for himself. Jacobs, who is working toward achieving even higher goals, will remain an industry trendsetter for years to come.

Whenever there are rumors that Karl Lagerfeld might retire as head designer and creative director for the fashion house Chanel, it's assumed Jacobs is after the job.

Chanel has been one of the world's most sought-after fashion brands since it was founded by Gabrielle "Coco" Chanel in 1909. She captured the world's attention with modern jersey sweaters, beaded dresses, and even pants for women—something that was decidedly against cultural norms at the time. In 1921, she introduced Chanel No. 5, which went on to become one of the best-selling fragrances of all time. Lagerfeld joined the fashion house in 1983, adding glamour and sexiness to its classic collections.

For his part, Jacobs has repeatedly said the Chanel position would be a dream come true. "Chanel would be the scariest job in the world to get, but it would also be the coup de grace," he told *New York* magazine in 2005. "I'd be scared to death and thrilled, but it's the only thing I'd love to do other than what I'm doing right now. If that's all that's left, that's not such a bad thing. Karl's (Lagerfeld) the perfect person for the job and he's not going anywhere, but if there's anything that tickles me behind the ear once in a while, that's it. That's the only, the ultimate thing."

ELEMENTS OF STYLE

I'm making clothes because I love it. I enjoy it—despite the problems, the fires, the backers, late deliveries, the customs. I love it, and the minute I stop loving it, nobody's gonna buy this stuff, because it is my energy, my enthusiasm that people are responding to.

—*Marc Jacobs in* Women's Wear Daily, *1988*

I don't think it's in me to do great evening gowns. If I had that ability I'd probably be cranking them out, but I don't really think it comes very naturally to me. I like a pretty dress but I'm not very good at a grand entrance or exit maker. It's just not something I feel. So it would be very forced.

—*Marc Jacobs in* Women's Wear Daily, *2004*

Any creative choice isn't done by math or focus groups. You do something that has integrity and you make creative choices, and you get it out there and see what happens.

—*Marc Jacobs in* Women's Wear Daily, *2007*

For now, though, Jacobs seems quite content to continue his roles at Louis Vuitton and Marc Jacobs. "Even in every designer's life, whatever scale they grow to be, there's this sort of period where they're on everybody's lips or on a certain group of people's lips," he told *Women's Wear Daily* in 2004. "So, we want to do as much as we can within our time. We just hope to keep going. . . . But it's out of our hands once we've done the creative work and Robert has placed it in stores and we've all fought and done our part. Then it's got to become somewhat organic, like people have to like it and buy it."

Continuing to produce the "it" shows and continuing to design the "must-have" shirt or shoe is Jacobs's long-term priority. As French fashion designer Coco Chanel once famously said, "I want to be part of what is going to happen."

Jacobs lives—and works—by that same motto every day.

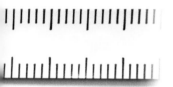 

Chronology

1963	Born April 9 in New York City.
1970	Jacobs's father dies.
1984	Graduates from Parsons the New School for Design in New York City, winning three of the school's most prestigious awards.
1987	Jacobs's paternal grandmother, whom he credits for raising him, dies.
	Jacobs becomes the youngest designer ever to be awarded the Council of Fashion Designers of

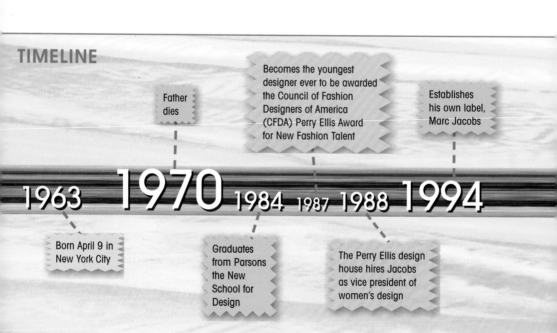

TIMELINE

Father dies

Becomes the youngest designer ever to be awarded the Council of Fashion Designers of America (CFDA) Perry Ellis Award for New Fashion Talent

Establishes his own label, Marc Jacobs

1963 1970 1984 1987 1988 1994

Born April 9 in New York City

Graduates from Parsons the New School for Design

The Perry Ellis design house hires Jacobs as vice president of women's design

America (CFDA) Perry Ellis Award for New Fashion Talent.

1988	The Perry Ellis design house hires Jacobs and business partner Robert Duffy as vice president of women's design and president respectively.
1992	Shows a grunge-inspired collection for Perry Ellis featuring Doc Martens and cartoon T-shirts. Critics love it; The company fires him.
1994	Establishes his own label, Marc Jacobs.
1997	Hired as creative director of Louis Vuitton.
2000	Jacobs enters rehab to address drug and alcohol addictions.
2001	Partners with 1980s designer Stephen Sprouse to update Vuitton's classic "Speedy" bag; the graffiti-inspired look is a huge success, which translates to shoes, luggage, and scarves.

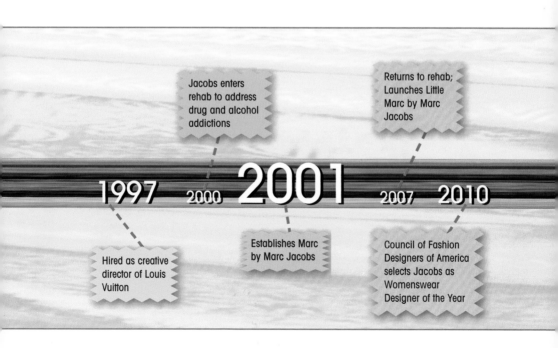

Jacobs enters rehab to address drug and alcohol addictions

Returns to rehab; Launches Little Marc by Marc Jacobs

1997   2000   **2001**   2007   2010

Hired as creative director of Louis Vuitton

Establishes Marc by Marc Jacobs

Council of Fashion Designers of America selects Jacobs as Womenswear Designer of the Year

Establishes a more youthful line, Marc by Marc Jacobs.

2007   Returns to rehab and then spends a year in the gym, transforming his body.

Launches Little Marc by Marc Jacobs, a line of children's clothing and accessories.

2008   Pays cash settlements in response to separate allegations of plagiarism and bribery.

2010   Council of Fashion Designers of America selects Jacobs as Womenswear Designer of the Year; it is Jacobs's ninth CFDA award.

Glossary

absinthe   A green liqueur known for its bitter taste and high alcohol content.

apathy   Lack of emotion or feeling.

astute   Keenly aware and intelligent.

balked   Refused abruptly.

brokered   Managed or negotiated contracts, purchases, or sales.

cashmere   Soft fabric made from the fine, downy wool growing beneath the outer hair of the cashmere goat.

collaborations   Objects created by working jointly with another or others.

commissioned   Placed an order for.

copyright   The legal right granted to an author, designer, composer, or creator to exclusive publication, production, sale, and distribution of a particular artistic work.

crinolines   Petticoats made of a stiff fabric of cotton or horsehair, used to stiffen or add volume to garments.

duty-free   Exempt from customs fees.

egotism   An inflated sense of one's own importance.

eminent   Noteworthy; standing above the others.

imploded   Violently collapsed inward.

infrastructure   The foundation or systems needed to run an organization or business.

machismo   An exaggerated sense of strength or toughness.

melancholy   Affected with depression or sadness.

monogram   A design composed of one or more letters, typically the initials of a name.

paparazzi   Photographers who doggedly pursue celebrities to take candid pictures to sell to magazines and newspapers.

plagiarism   Taking someone else's designs, words, or ideas and presenting them as one's own.

portfolio   A collection of materials that are representative of a person's work.

prolific   Producing abundant works or results.

rehabilitation   Treatment through which one is restored to good health.

sustainability   Using a resource so that it is not depleted or permanently damaged; meeting current needs without compromising the ability of future generations to meet their own needs.

vaudeville   A type of entertainment prevalent onstage in the United States and Canada from the early 1880s until the early 1930s; acts included dancers, musicians, comedians, trained animals, magicians, and more.

Alexander, Hilary. "New York Fashion Week: In the Front Row." *Telegraph* (September 12, 2007).

———. "Marc Jacobs Talks About New Louis Vuitton Store." *Telegraph* (May 26, 2010).

Armstrong, Lisa. "Marc Jacobs: The King of Fashion Bares All." *Financial Times* (September 8, 2008).

Bagley, Christopher. "Marc Jacobs: Long Intimidated by the Art World, Marc Jacobs Didn't Start Collecting Until Five Years Ago—and Now He Just Can't Stop; Inside the Designer's Paris Apartment." *W* (November 2007).

Beckham, Victoria. "The 2010 *Time* 100: Marc Jacobs." *Time* (April 29, 2010).

Betts, Kate. "Downsizing Style." *Time* (January 17, 2008).

Binkley, Christina. "Life After the First Lady: Jason Wu's Show Reveals His New, Post-Obama Ambitions." *Wall Street Journal* (September 11, 2009).

Borden, Mark. "Managing Marc Jacobs." *Fortune* (September 11, 2007).

The Charlie Rose Show. "Marc Jacobs." PBS Television. February 19, 1998.

———. "Charlie Rose Green Room—Marc Jacobs." PBS Television. June 11, 2008.

Clarke, Mary. "Marc Jacobs." *Index* (2001).

Cotton Incorporated. "Star Light, Star Bright: Never Underestimate the Power of Politicos and Celebrities," press release, October 23, 2008. Available online. URL: http://www.cottoninc.com/PressReleases/?articleID=483.

Craik, Laura. "How the King of Grunge Became a $1.2 Billion Man: He's the Man Who Turned Around Louis Vuitton—but Don't Forget His

Other Labels; With Six Collections a Year, Is Marc Jacobs the Most Wanted Man in Fashion?" *Evening Standard* (April 19, 2001).

Foley, Bridget, with contributions from Marc Karimzadeh. "Jacobs Blasts Back: Designer Tells Critics Shut Up or Stay Home." *Women's Wear Daily* (September 13, 2007).

Fox, Imogen. "Marc Jacobs: One of the Great Contemporary Fashion Talents . . . He Can Pin Down Cool Again and Again Without Being Alienating." *Guardian* (September 26, 2008).

Freeman, Hadley. "Marc Jacobs Tumbles off His Pedestal at the Paris Shows." *Guardian* (October 11, 2007).

Friedman, Vanessa. "Lunch with the FT: Marc Jacobs." *Financial Times* (May 21, 2010).

Grigoriadis, Vanessa. "The Deep Shallowness of Marc Jacobs." *Rolling Stone* (November 27, 2008).

Han, Phil. "Naomi Campbell: 'I Had to Look in the Mirror and Face My Demons.'" CNN, February 15, 2010. Available online. URL: http://articles.cnn.com/2010-02-15/entertainment/naomi.campbell.supermodel.violence_1_assaulting=supermodel=naomi=campbell.demons?_s=PM:SHOWBIZ

Hicklin, Aaron. "Marc Jacobs as You've Never Seen Him Before." *Out* (September 2007).

Horyn, Cathy. "The Handbag Gets the Last Word." *New York Times* (October 8, 2007).

———. "Marc Jacobs: Now Man." *New York Times* (September 14, 2009).

Huckbody, Jamie. "Interview: Marc Jacobs." *Harper's Bazaar* (August 19, 2009).

Jacobs, Marc. Comment on "Alaia: Burning the Midnight Oil." *New York Times*, On the Runway Blog (October 9, 2007).

Karimzadeh, Marc, Stephanie D. Smith, Irin Carmon, Amy Wicks, Nick Axelrod, and Rosemary Feitelberg. "Memo Pad: Outside the Box." *Women's Wear Daily* (January 11, 2008).

LaFerla, Ruth. "Online, Feisty Critics." *New York Times* (September 8, 2005).

Larocca, Amy. "Lost and Found: Marc Jacobs Is Fashion's Awkward, Lonely Outsider; Marc Jacobs Is Fashion's Coolest, Most Influential

Designer; The Paradoxical Triumph of a Lost City Boy." *New York Times Magazine* (August 21, 2005).

———. "Daily Intel: Marc Jacobs Goes to Rehab." *New York Times* (March 12, 2007).

———. "Straight Shooter." *New York Times Magazine* (August 17, 2008).

———. "Marc Jacobs Exposes the Latest 'It' Bag." *Harper's Bazaar* (October 2008).

Lau, Venessa. "Marc Jacobs on Fashion and Francophilia," WWDBlogs, March 24, 2010. Available online. URL: http://www.wwd.com/fashion-blogs/marc_jacobs_on_fashion_and_fra-10-03.

Levy, Ariel. "Enchanted: The Transformation of Marc Jacobs." *New Yorker* (September 1, 2008).

———. "Fashion Designer Marc Jacobs Reveals All." *Telegraph* (January 2, 2009).

Lipke, David. "Marc Jacobs Wins CFDA's Top Men's Award; Ralph Lauren and Sean John Are Edged Out Despite Recent Raves for Their Collections." *Harrisonburg (Va.) Daily News Record* (June 10, 2002).

Martin, J.J. "Marc on Top." *Harper's Bazaar* (2007).

Menkes, Suzy. "Marc Jacobs's Recipe for Success." *New York Times* (February 6, 2006).

New Straits Times. "Steven Meisel Shoots Madonna." (December 7, 2008).

New York Times. "The Cut: Critics Hail Marchesa and Marc by Marc Jacobs" (February 7, 2008).

New York Times Magazine. "Marc Jacobs Thrills Critics; Carolina Herrera 'Confounds'" (September 15, 2009).

O'Brien, Glenn. "Marc Jacobs." *Interview* (June 2008).

Out. "Out 100: Our Annual List of the Year's Most Interesting, Influential, and Newsworthy LGBT People" (2005).

Panter, Josh. "The Turning Point." *Elle* (March 2007).

Peden, Lauren David. "Marc by Marc Jacobs: Show Report." *Vogue UK* (February 5, 2008).

Reynolds, Cory. "Juergen Teller." *Index* (2000).

Rickey, Melanie. "Marc Jacobs: A Fashion Force to Be Reckoned With." *Independent* (May 26, 2008).

Seabrook, John. "A Samurai in Paris: Suzy Menkes," *New Yorker* (March 17, 2001).

Silva, Horacio. "On the Campaign Trail: Juergen Teller and Marc Jacobs." *New York Times Magazine* (September 1, 2009).

Socha, Miles. "Memo Pad: Madonna and Marc Jacobs." *Women's Wear Daily* (December 4, 2008).

Spindler, Amy. "Two Take the Money and Produce." *New York Times* (April 9, 1997).

Teen Vogue. *The Teen Vogue Handbook: An Insider's Guide to Careers in Fashion.* New York: Razorbill, 2009.

Trebay, Guy. "Familiar, but Not: Marc Jacobs and the Borrower's Art." *New York Times* (May 28, 2002).

Wilson, Eric. "Marc Jacobs: Seizing the Moment." *Women's Wear Daily* (November 17, 2004).

———. "Loving and Hating Marc Jacobs." *New York Times* (November 15, 2007).

Wiseman, Eve. "Marc Jacobs: A Designer with Bags of Talent." *Observer* (August 31, 2008).

Zinko, Carolyne. "Suzy Menkes Is all over the Map." *San Francisco Chronicle* (May 16, 2010).

Further Resources

BOOKS

Castets, Simon. *Louis Vuitton: Art, Fashion and Architecture*. New York: Rizzoli, 2009.

English, Bonnie. *Fashion: The 50 Most Influential Fashion Designers of All Time*. New York: Barron's, 2010.

Fitzgerald, Tracy, Adrian Grandon, and Steven Faerm. *200 Projects to Get You into Fashion Design*. Hauppauge, N.Y.: Barron's, 2009.

Jacobs, Marc, and Bridget Foley. *Marc Jacobs*. New York: Assouline, 2007.

Pasols, Paul-Gérard. *Louis Vuitton: The Birth of Modern Luxury*. New York: Harry N. Abrams, 2005.

Teller, Juergen, and Marc Jacobs. *Marc Jacobs Advertising, 1998–2009*. Göttingen, Germany: Steidl, 2009.

WEB SITES

Council of Fashion Designers of America
www.cfda.com

Louis Vuitton
www.louisvuitton.com

Marc Jacobs
www.marcjacobs.com

Mercedes-Benz New York Fashion Week
www.mbfashionweek.com

Parsons the New School for Design
www.newschool.edu/parsons

Picture Credits

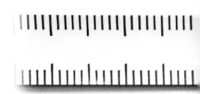

Index

About the Author

MARY BOONE has written 17 books for young readers, including biographies about Pink, Akon, Justin Bieber, and 50 Cent. She worked for several midwestern newspapers and still remembers the thrill of long ago interviewing Marc Jacobs while working as a fashion editor at one of those papers. Boone now lives in Tacoma, Washington, with her husband, Mitch, and kids, Eve and Eli.